AS/A-LEVEL YEAR 1

STUDENT GUIDE

AQA

Business

Topics 1.1–1.3

What is business?

Managers, leadership and decision-making

Decision-making to improve marketing performance

Neil James

Original edition: Isobel Rollitt-James

PHILIP ALLAN FOR
HODDER
EDUCATION
AN HACHETTE UK COMPANY

Philip Allan, an imprint of Hodder Education, an Hachette UK company, Blenheim Court, George Street, Banbury, Oxfordshire OX16 5BH

Orders

Bookpoint Ltd, 130 Milton Park, Abingdon, Oxfordshire OX14 4SB

tel: 01235 827827

fax: 01235 400401

e-mail: education@bookpoint.co.uk

Lines are open 9.00 a.m.–5.00 p.m., Monday to Saturday, with a 24-hour message answering service. You can also order through the Hodder Education website: www.hoddereducation. co.uk

© Neil James 2015

ISBN 978-1-4718-4326-6

First printed 2015

Impression number 5 4 3 2 1

Year 2019 2018 2017 2016 2015

This Guide has been written specifically to support students preparing for the AQA AS and A-level Business (Topics 1.1–1.3) examinations. The content has been neither approved nor endorsed by AQA and remains the sole responsibility of the author.

Typeset by Integra Software Services Pvt. Ltd., Pondicherry, India

Cover photo: Giuseppe Porzani/Fotolia

Printed in Italy

Hachette UK's policy is to use papers that are natural, renewable and recyclable products and made from wood grown in sustainable forests. The logging and manufacturing processes are expected to conform to the environmental regulations of the country of origin.

Contents

Content Guidance

Questions & Answers

■Getting the most from this book

Exam tips

Advice on key points in the text to help you learn and recall content, avoid pitfalls, and polish your exam technique in order to boost your grade.

Knowledge check

Rapid-fire questions throughout the Content Guidance section to check your understanding.

Knowledge check answers

1 Turn to the back of the book for the Knowledge check answers.

Summaries

■ Each core topic is rounded off by a bullet-list summary for quick-check reference of what you need to know.

Exam-style questions

Commentary on the questions

Tips on what you need to do to gain full marks, indicated by the icon **e**

Sample student answers

Practise the questions, then look at the student answers that follow.

Commentary on sample student answers

Find out how many marks each answer would be awarded in the exam and then read the comments (preceded by the icon **e**) following each student answer. Annotations that link back to points made in the student answers show exactly how and where marks are gained or lost.

Questions & Answers

(c) Analyse the potential benefits to Trumps Travel of Andy's style of leadership. [9 marks]

e It is important that students only develop the benefits of this leadership style and not the drawbacks.

(d) To what extent do you believe Andy's use of a decision tree to be effective in deciding who should develop the new website? Using evidence from the case study justify your view. [15 marks]

e 'To what extent' means to make a judgement. The reasons for and against the effectiveness of decision trees in this case can be put forward and an overall justified conclusion made.

(e) Andy believes that the external environment is the key influence on his decision-making. To what extent to you agree? Justify your view. [16 marks]

e This is a broad question and the key to answering it is to be selective. Which of the external environment factors would have most influence on Trumps Travel? Perhaps look at two areas as well as another non-external factor before coming to a justified conclusion.

Student A

(a) The role of a leader is to analyse situations, set objectives, make decisions and review the situation. It is important for Trumps Travel that Andy can do this as the business is struggling and he needs to analyse why, and make decisions in order to revive its position. This is what he has been appointed for.

e 4/4 marks awarded. This is a good answer. The role of a leader is clearly identified and set in the context of Trumps Travel.

(b) The Tannenbaum Schmidt continuum and the Blake Mouton grid are both models of leadership. On the Tannenbaum Schmidt continuum, Andy is very much on the left-hand side, telling people what to do. Although he lets others have their say, he is the one who decides — once he has made up his mind that is it. On the Blake Mouton grid he probably falls into task management as he is more concerned with the end result rather than the people he is working with. He does let them have a say, but his decision is final.

e 6/6 marks awarded. A good answer — there is no doubt that this student understands these two models of leadership and evidence from the case is used to place Andy's style within each.

(c) Andy's style of leadership appears to be autocratic, which can be useful in some situations. Decision-making is likely to be quick as there are no committees and lengthy discussions. The situation is assessed by the leader and the decision made. Trumps Travel is obviously undergoing difficult times and it needs to make decisions quickly otherwise the situation will only get worse and it will fall further behind the competition. Therefore, this style could be good for the business.

68   AQA Business

■ About this book

This Student Guide 1, together with its companion Student Guide 2, has been written with one thing in mind: to provide you with the ideal resource for your revision of both AQA AS Business (7131) and the first year of AQA A-level Business (7132). In your study of the subject you will look at business in a variety of contexts, small and large, national and global, service and manufacturing.

The overall focus of the AS Business and first year of the A-level specifications is decision-making in the various functional areas, the influences on those decisions and the impact they may have on stakeholders. Central to these specifications are the following themes:

- How developments in technology are affecting decisions in the functional areas.
- The influence of ethical and environmental issues on decisions in the functional areas.
- How decision-making in the various functional areas improves competitiveness.
- The interrelationship between decision-making in the various functional areas.

The focus of Student Guide 1 is the following:

- What a business is, its nature and purpose, its different forms and the external environment in which it operates.
- Management, leadership and decision-making, together with the role of stakeholders.
- Decision-making to improve marketing performance.

Content Guidance

The Content Guidance section offers concise coverage combining an overview of key terms and concepts with identification of opportunities for you to illustrate higher level skills of analysis and evaluation.

Questions & Answers

The Questions & Answers section provides examples of the various types of questions with which you are likely to be faced, such as multiple choice, short-answer, data response and case studies (Student Guide 2 only) and, for A-level only, essay questions. There is also a section on quantitative skills question practice that provides additional examples of the type of calculations you are likely to be faced with. The multiple-choice and short-answer questions focus on the broad content of this guide and the five data-response questions focus on specific aspects of content. Student Guide 2 has one case study question that provides a much broader approach to the complete AS specification.

The questions in this guide are tailored so that you can apply your learning while the topic is still fresh in your mind, either during the course itself or when you have revised a topic in preparation for the exam. Together with the sample answers, this should provide you with a sound basis for sitting your exams in Business.

Content Guidance

This section outlines the following areas of the AS Business and first year of the A-level Business specifications:

- What is business?
- Managers, leadership and decision-making
- Decision-making to improve marketing performance

Read through the topic area before attempting a question from the Questions & Answers section.

■ What is business?

Understanding the nature and purpose of business

Why businesses exist

A business is any organisation set up to service or satisfy the wants and needs of people. There are a number of reasons for setting up a business, including to provide:

- goods and services (including **public services**)
- money for owners (profit)
- help and support for others (charitable organisations)

Public services
Services provided by the government or local authority, for example the NHS, police force, fire service and rubbish collection. (See p. 8 for more information on the public sector.)

The relationship between mission and objectives

An organisation's mission statement gives the big picture of the business and represents its vision, core purpose and values. It is sometimes seen as the philosophy that guides how a business operates. For example, Tesco's mission statement is: 'We make what matters better, together', whereas Sainsbury's is: 'Our mission is to be the consumer's first choice for food, delivering products of outstanding quality and great service at a competitive cost through working faster, simpler and together'.

Therefore, the mission statement paints the broad picture, whereas the business's objectives are more specific; they are targets or goals that will enable an organisation to achieve its overall mission. In other words, the mission statement gives a direction or focus for the objectives that have been set and, by having objectives, a business can work toward achieving its mission.

As well as overall business objectives, each functional area of a business has its own set of objectives enabling it to contribute to the overall business objectives and mission.

Knowledge check 1

Write down three reasons why businesses exist.

Knowledge check 2

Briefly outline the difference between the mission statement and objectives.

All objectives must be **SMART**:

Specific   Each objective must be clear, precise and well defined.

Measurable   It must be possible to determine when an objective has been completed.

Achievable   Each objective must be within the business's capabilities and have sufficient resources.

Realistic   Each objective must be challenging but possible to achieve given the capabilities and resources.

Time-based   There must be a deadline to work to.

For example, increasing sales revenue by 5% in the next year is a SMART objective, whereas simply having an objective to increase sales is not.

The relative importance of different objectives is likely to vary over time depending on circumstances. In difficult economic times, survival is likely to be more important than profit or environmental targets. However, in a booming economy profit, growth and social issues will take on a far more important role.

Exam tip

The relative importance of business objectives change over time and depend on the individual business and the circumstances in which it is operating.

Common business objectives

The overall business objectives are targets that have been set for the whole business and are often referred to as *corporate objectives*. These might include:

- profit — this is vital for the long-term health and security of a business
- growth — this might be in terms of market share or sales turnover, although for smaller businesses such as a small corner shop or a plumber this may be less of an issue
- survival — this is important for many businesses in times of economic uncertainty and for all businesses when first starting out
- cash flow — for many smaller businesses, cash flow may be more important than profit
- customer service — if a business is to gain loyal customers in a competitive marketplace, good customer service is essential

Knowledge check 3

What is meant when we say that all business objectives should be SMART?

Over recent years **corporate social responsibility (CSR)** has come to play an increasingly important role and as a result many businesses are setting themselves social and ethical objectives. This relates to how a business treats its workers and suppliers and the environment, including the use of sweatshops, fair trade and pollution.

Why businesses set objectives

Having objectives is important for the business and each functional area for a number of reasons:

- Objectives give meaning to planning and enable the business to remain focused.
- The business can measure and review performance. As a result, its objectives may be revised or corrective action may be taken, depending on the circumstances.
- Objectives provide a motivation for those responsible for implementing plans.

Corporate social responsibility (CSR)
A company's sense of responsibility towards the community and the environment in which it operates.

The measurement and importance of profit

Profit is the reward the owners of a business receive for taking the risk of setting up in business. Without profit as an incentive, there would be a general reluctance to set up in business. Profit is calculated as:

profit = revenue − total costs

Revenue (also known as turnover, sales or sales turnover) is the money received by a business from the sales of its products or services. It is calculated as:

revenue = price per unit × number of units sold (output)

Total costs are the value of all business costs and may be split into fixed and variable costs:

- *fixed costs* are those that do not change with output, rent, rates, insurance premiums etc.
- *variable costs* are those that vary directly with output, raw materials, direct labour etc.

Therefore:

total costs = fixed costs + variable costs

Opportunities for analysis

- The benefits and drawbacks of mission statements.
- The reasons for a particular business setting objectives.
- The reasons why objectives might change over time.

Opportunities for evaluation

- The relative importance of different objectives as circumstances change.
- The extent to which profit is a measure of the size of a business.
- The relative importance of profit to a particular business.

Understanding different business forms

Private sector and public sector

In the UK there are a number of different forms of business, but before we look at these it is necessary to distinguish between the private sector and the public sector.

The *private sector* is that part of the economy where a business is owned and controlled by an individual or a group of individuals. There are number of different types of business in the private sector such as sole traders, partnerships, private limited companies, public limited companies, charities and mutuals.

The *public sector* is that part of the economy that is owned and controlled by the government or local authorities. In the UK this means a number of the public services such as the police force, fire service, the BBC and the NHS, as well as local council-run services such as rubbish collection. The public sector used to

Profit The reward the owners of a business receive for taking the risk of setting up in business.

Exam tip

Business is examined largely through case studies, so your answers should be linked specifically to the business in the case study This is the skill of application.

Privatisation The process of transferring ownership of government-owned and controlled industries or businesses to the private sector.

include a number of key nationalised industries and utilities such as coal, steel, water and telephone, but these have largely been sold off to the private sector through a privatisation process.

Sole traders and partnerships

These are unincorporated businesses, meaning there is no distinction in law between the owner and the business itself. They represent the simplest forms of business and are relatively straightforward to set up, but as the owners have unlimited liability they are totally responsible for the debts of the business. Typical examples include small shop-keepers, plumbers, joiners and electricians.

Advantages
- They are easy to set up with few legal formalities.
- The owner takes all the profit.
- They have financial privacy as their financial affairs do not have to be published.
- They have greater independence than other legal structures and as a result may be more responsive to changes in circumstance.

Disadvantages
- They have unlimited liability so the owner's personal assets may be used in the event of failure.
- They have limited capital and access to capital (loans) for expansion.
- Their business skills may be limited.
- Problems may arise if the owner is ill or wishes to take a holiday.

Private limited companies (Ltd)

Private limited companies have at least two owners (shareholders) and are incorporated businesses under the Companies Act. They have limited liability, which means the owners are liable (responsible) only for the money they have invested or agreed to invest in the business and their own personal assets cannot be used to pay business debts. Shares do not trade on the stock exchange. Generally, private limited companies are small to medium-sized businesses that are family owned. There are, however, some well-known examples including Clarks (shoes), Baxters (soups and preserves) and Walkers Shortbread (biscuits).

Advantages
- The owners have limited liability so their personal assets cannot be taken in the event of failure.
- They have access to a greater amount of capital.
- They have greater privacy than public limited companies.
- They have less pressure from outside investors and greater flexibility.

Disadvantages
- They are more difficult to set up than unincorporated businesses, with more formalities and associated costs.
- Although access to capital may be greater than unincorporated businesses, it is still less than public limited companies.
- Financial information is accessible by outsiders.

Unincorporated businesses Those where there is no distinction in law between the individual owner and the business itself.

Knowledge check 4

Identify three advantages of being a sole trader.

Incorporated businesses Those that have a legal identity separate from the individual owners. This means that the owners have limited liability and are not responsible personally for the debts of the business.

Knowledge check 5

What is the difference between an incorporated business and an unincorporated business?

Public limited companies (plc)

Public limited companies are owned by shareholders who have limited liability, but anyone can buy shares through the stock market and become a part owner. A shareholder is entitled to a share of the profits in the business, but the amount given is decided by the directors and is known as a dividend. Using the share price it is also possible to work out the total value of a business or market capitalisation (share price × number of shares issued). Although there are some large and well-known private limited companies, public limited companies tend to be the largest. This is because they have access to larger amounts of capital through the stock market and the issue of shares. Examples include BP, Shell, Marks and Spencer, and Next.

Advantages

- The shareholders have limited liability so their personal assets cannot be used if the business fails.
- They have access to greater amounts of capital.
- They have greater power over suppliers regarding credit terms.

Disadvantages

- They have to publish greater amounts of financial detail leading to more scrutiny of their affairs.
- The original owners are likely to lose control of the business.
- Pressure from investors may result in greater emphasis on short-term profit rather than long-term performance.

Exam tip

When discussing limited liability in answers, always relate to the business in question. Why would that business benefit from limited liability?

Non-profit organisations

Other types of organisation in the private sector are non-profit organisations such as charities and mutuals. *Charities* may be large fund-raising organisations such as Cancer Research, Winston's Wish or the Red Cross, or they may be smaller charitable trusts designed to manage assets such as money, investments or land. *Mutuals* are interesting as they are generally private businesses whose ownership base is made up of its clients and policy holders, for example insurance companies and some building societies. Although both these examples have traditionally been organised in this way, many big insurance companies and building societies have tended to become public limited companies.

Knowledge check 6

What do you understand by the term 'mutual'?

Reasons for choosing different forms of business

Business owners have to choose the structure that will best meet their needs. The choice of business structure depends on a number of factors:

- the potential risks and liabilities of a business — the greater the risk and liabilities, the greater the need for incorporation and limited liability
- the product or service being offered — the more risky the product or service, the greater the need for incorporation
- the formalities and expenses of setting up — sole traders are easy to set up with few formalities and costs, so unless a business is particularly risky or requires access to large amounts of capital an unincorporated business would probably be appropriate

Exam tip

When deciding on the most appropriate legal structure for a business, base any recommendation on the circumstances of the individual business, its size, the product or service and the risk involved.

Reasons for changing business form

- A change in circumstances, such as the growth of a business, may mean that the owner wishes to incorporate their business in order to benefit from limited liability.
- The owner may find it easier to raise capital by becoming incorporated or, in the case of a private limited company, by changing it to a public limited company.
- Acquisition or takeover may cause a change of structure, for example a private limited company may be taken over by a public limited company.
- Sometimes a business may move from being public limited to private limited in order to distance itself from the constant scrutiny of the City. One example of this is Richard Branson's Virgin.

The role of shareholders and why they invest

Individuals can invest in public limited companies to become shareholders and part owners of the business. As shareholders they have certain rights and a role to play in the running of the business.

Major decisions that will have an impact on shareholders are required to be approved by them at a general meeting called by the directors. Their main role therefore is to attend this meeting and discuss whatever is on the agenda, ensuring the directors do not go beyond their powers. There are also certain things that can be done only by shareholders such as the removal of directors or changing the name of a company. In practice, for individual shareholders this means very little as they normally own only a small proportion of the issued shares. The biggest shareholders in public limited companies are usually financial institutions, pension funds, insurance companies etc.

People invest in shares primarily for two reasons:

- *Income*. Shareholders are entitled to a share of company profits — the amount given is decided by the board of directors and can vary, but investors would hope that the return they receive (the **dividend**) will increase over time.
- *Capital growth*. Shareholders hope that the value of their shares will increase over time.

Influences on share price and the significance of share price changes

The share price of any company can, however, fluctuate both positively and negatively. This can be for a number of reasons:

- performance — better or worse than expected profits
- expectation — of better or worse profit performance
- changes — within the market or competitive environment
- world uncertainty — such as conflict in the Middle East

Market capitalisation is calculated as:

market capitalisation = share price × number of shares issued

It therefore gives a valuation of the company — its net worth. Changes in the share price therefore affect the valuation of the business. A falling share price might provide an opportunity for investment or takeover, or it might be an indication of a business in decline.

Knowledge check 7

List three things that might influence the choice of legal structure for a business.

Dividend A share of the after-tax profit of a company distributed to its shareholders according to the number of shares held.

Knowledge check 8

Identify three factors that might cause a company's share price to fall.

Market capitalisation This is calculated using the formula: share price × number of shares issued.

The effects of ownership on mission, objectives, decisions and performance

Outline briefly what is meant by 'market capitalisation'.

Public limited companies are owned by shareholders who are driven by profit, which can lead to a short-term approach to business. Decision-making may be made more on the basis of achieving profit and the philosophy outlined in the mission statement often takes a 'back seat'. This emphasis on profit was demonstrated by Tesco in autumn 2014 when it was shown to have made mistakes in reporting profits higher than they actually were. These failings led to a big fall in Tesco's share price. Sole traders and private limited companies are less affected by this need to achieve profits and may be able to keep a closer focus on their mission statement and objectives.

Opportunities for analysis

- Why a particular business might seek incorporation.
- The impact of a change of ownership/structure on mission and objectives.
- Analysis of the reasons for investing in a particular business.

Opportunities for evaluation

- Justification of adopting one form of business structure over an alternative form.
- The implications of changing the legal structure of a business.
- Judgement on how becoming a public limited company and having shareholders might change the objectives and performance of a business.

Understanding that businesses operate within an external environment

Businesses do not operate in a vacuum and are subject to influences from the external environment that will have an impact on demand costs and the way it operates in general.

How the external environment can affect costs and demand

External influences on a business can impact on its ability to achieve its strategic goals and objectives. By external it means they are beyond the control of the business and include competition, market conditions, economic factors, demographic factors and environmental issues. Such factors can affect both demand for a product or service and the costs of operating a business. Some of these influences are unpredictable, whereas some influences change regularly, but whatever the case a business is likely to have to take action to cope. The effect might be positive or negative.

Exam tip

Don't assume that the influence of the external environment will always be negative; it can also be positive. Examine the circumstances of the business in any stimulus material in order to decide whether it is positive or negative.

Competition

As *monopolies* are illegal in the UK, all businesses face competition from others offering a similar or the same product. If an individual business differentiates its product from that of its competitors with a **unique selling point** (USP), it might be able to increase demand. Alternatively, if its competitor releases a new, more technologically advanced, product or additional facilities, demand could fall. If the products are relatively the same such as in the grocery market, there will be pressure to reduce price and lower costs in order to maintain profitability.

Market conditions

Market conditions are the characteristics of a market into which a business is entering or into which a new product is being introduced. Such characteristics might be the number of competitors, the intensity of competitiveness and the markets' growth rate. A market with high market growth and a low intensity of competitiveness is likely to present greater opportunities for higher demand than the opposite.

Economic factors

This might include the stage of the economic cycle, interest rates, inflation and exchange rates. It is interest rates that are the focus of the AS specification. A change in the interest rate can have a big impact on business for a number of reasons.

First, it has a direct impact on the costs of a business if it has borrowed money or intends to borrow in the future. A rise in the interest rate is likely to lead to rise in costs and a fall in interest rates to a fall in costs. In terms of decision-making, it is cheaper to borrow at times of low interest rates and the level of rates and their expected level is likely to be a key influence on decisions to invest.

Second, the level of interest rates can affect demand: rising interest rates could mean lower demand as consumers who have borrowed money could be facing higher interest payments and have less disposable income as a result. Other consumers might also be encouraged to save more because of rising interest rates. Falling interest rates are likely to have the opposite effect.

Finally, if a business has large cash reserves it could benefit from rising interest rates because of the higher interest received.

Demographic factors

Demographic factors refer to socio-economic characteristics of the population such as age, sex, income and occupation by which a business might segment the market, as well as birth and death rates, the level of public health and immigration. All of these factors may have an influence on the level of demand of a business and the type of products and services on offer. This can be illustrated by the development of push-button hand brakes, reversing sensors and cameras in cars, which can to some extent

Unique selling point
A real or perceived benefit of a good or service that differentiates it from competing brands and gives its buyer a logical reason to prefer it over other brands.

Knowledge check 10

Briefly outline how a business might benefit positively from a fall in interest rates.

be attributed to an ageing population as they make life easier for elderly drivers and may therefore keep them driving for longer, helping sales of cars.

Environmental issues and fair trade

Environmental issues cover a broad area and can have a big impact on the way a business operates and its costs of production, as well as potentially influencing consumer demand. No longer can a business carry out production without regard for its local environment. Any hint of *pollution* in the UK is quickly brought to the public attention through social media, for example, and pressure groups can have a significant impact on the business. Businesses therefore sometimes have to spend large amounts on measures to ensure that water, air and the surrounding countryside are kept free from pollution.

The concern for the environment is, to some extent, being driven by factors such as *global warming* and sustainable development. There is concern that carbon emissions are a contributing factor to global warming and that not only businesses but also governments should be doing more to cut carbon emissions. There is also a worry that certain resources are running out and so we should try to conserve and sustain resources. For example, the fishing industry is subject to quotas and some paper manufacturers now say they plant one new tree for every one they cut down.

Fair trade is about better prices, decent working conditions and fair terms of trade for farmers and workers in developing countries. This is likely to mean higher costs for a business, but it could lead to greater demand and a better reputation, as well as acting as a unique selling point.

These external factors can have a significant impact on the demand for products and services provided, the costs incurred and any profit made. Although a business might sometimes be caught out by sudden changes in the external environment (for example, the global recession of 2008 and its depth), it should be able to anticipate and plan for some changes. For example, demographic changes can be identified, changes in interest rates anticipated and new products and services provided in order to stay ahead of competitors. As a result, any negative impact on cost and demand may be minimised and any positive impact maximised.

Opportunities for analysis

- Discussion of how changing interest rates might affect a particular business.
- Analysis of a particular business's response to an ageing population.
- Analysis of why a business may decide to introduce fair-trade products.

Opportunities for evaluation

- The extent to which adopting environmental policies may affect the profit of a business.
- Evaluation of whether adopting environmental policies is the right decision for a particular business.

Sustainable development Where a business aims to meet the needs of the present without compromising the ability of future generations to meet its own needs.

Knowledge check 11

Why might a business adopt a fair-trade approach?

Summary

- Businesses exist to make a profit, to provide goods and services, and to provide help and support to others.
- Businesses are likely to have both a mission statement and objectives.
- Mission statements represent the broad picture or vision of a business, whereas objectives are targets that enable the business to achieve its overall mission.
- Business objectives are set for a number of reasons: they provide a means of focus, a method for evaluating performance and can be motivating for employees. This is possible because objectives set should be SMART.
- Profit is the reward for taking risk and is calculated as total revenue minus total cost.
- Private-sector businesses, which are owned and controlled by individuals or groups of individuals, include sole traders, partnerships, private limited companies, public limited companies, and non-profit organisations such as charities and mutuals.
- Sole traders and partnerships are unincorporated and have unlimited liability, whereas private and public limited companies are incorporated and have limited liability.
- The public sector is owned and controlled by the government or local authorities.
- Owners of limited companies are known as shareholders.
- In a public limited company, share price × number of shares issued gives the market capitalisation of the business.
- Businesses operate within an external environment. This includes factors such as competition, market conditions, economic factors, demographic factors and environmental issues.

■ Managers, leadership and decision-making

Understanding management, leadership and decision-making

What managers do

In 1916, French engineer Henri Fayol created the first principles of the classical management theory. According to him, the five key functions of managers are to:

- draw up a *plan* of action
- *organise* work
- *command* people under them by giving instruction
- *coordinate* the resources for which they are responsible (for example, money, people or time)
- *control* activities and people by measuring and correcting them to enable performance to fit plans

The role of managers therefore includes setting objectives, analysing, making decisions, reviewing and leading.

Knowledge check 12

Outline briefly the role of a manager.

Types of management and leadership styles

In 1939 psychologist Kurt Lewin suggested three styles of leadership:

- *Autocratic*, where leaders make decisions without consultation. This style is good when quick decisions are needed and there is no need for team input, but it can be demotivating and lead to absenteeism and high turnover of labour.
- *Democratic*, where leaders make the final decision but include team members in the process. This style can lead to greater job satisfaction and productivity, but it can be slow and a hindrance if quick decisions are needed.
- *Laissez faire*, where team members are given freedom in how they work and setting of deadlines. Support is given, but otherwise leaders do not get involved. This style can be creative and give great job satisfaction, but it can also be damaging if team members lack the necessary skills and fail to work effectively.

In addition to the three main styles outlined above, leaders are also considered to belong to one of the following leadership groups:

- *Bureaucratic*, which tends to follow rules and procedures rigorously. This style is useful for work where safety is a key concern, but it is likely to lack flexibility, creativity and innovation.
- *Charismatic*, which revolves around a leader who is likely to inspire and motivate team members, but sometimes such leaders believe they are invincible and can do no wrong, which can be damaging to an organisation.

Two further studies on leadership styles involved the Tannenbaum Schmidt continuum and the Blake Mouton grid.

The Tannenbaum Schmidt continuum

This model shows where a manager's approach lies on a continuum, ranging from exerting rigid authority at one end ('Tells') through to the team having full freedom to act independently at the other end ('Delegates'), as shown in Figure 1.

Knowledge check 13

List three styles of leadership.

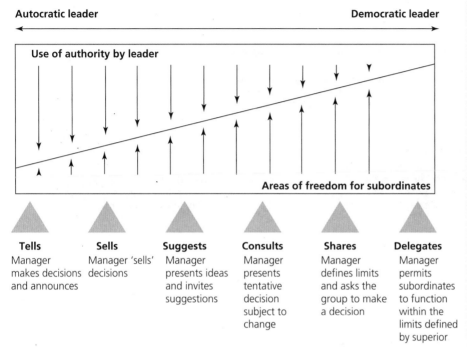

Autocratic leader — Democratic leader

Use of authority by leader

Areas of freedom for subordinates

Tells	Sells	Suggests	Consults	Shares	Delegates
Manager makes decisions and announces	Manager 'sells' decisions	Manager presents ideas and invites suggestions	Manager presents tentative decision subject to change	Manager defines limits and asks the group to make a decision	Manager permits subordinates to function within the limits defined by superior

Figure 1 The Tannenbaum Schmidt continuum

This shows the relationship between the level of freedom in decision-making a manager gives to a team of workers and the level of authority retained by the manager. As workers' freedom increases, so the manager's authority decreases.

The Blake Mouton grid

Developed in the 1960s by Robert Blake and Jane Mouton, this model portrays leadership through a grid depicting concern for people on the *y*-axis and concern for production on the *x*-axis, with each dimension ranging from 1 to 9, as shown in Figure 2.

The Blake Mouton grid results in five leadership styles:

- *country club management* — low task and high people orientation, believing this will increase motivation; lack of focus on tasks can hamper production
- *team management* — leaders focus on both people and task; emphasis on empowerment, trust and team-working
- *middle-of-the-road management* — leaders try to maintain balance between company goals and needs of people; likely to lead to average performance
- *impoverished management* — little concern for task or people; leaders are ineffective and organisation becomes disorganised
- *task management* — leaders have more concern for production than people, which may increase output in the short run but is likely to lead to high labour turnover

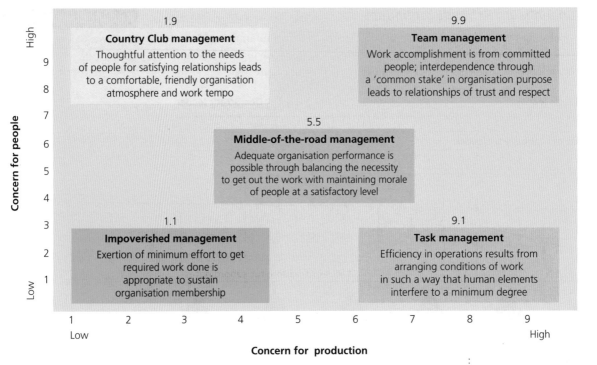

Figure 2 The Blake Mouton grid

The grid is useful in that it provides a framework to assess leadership styles, but it does not take into consideration individual business circumstances. Team management might appear from the grid to be the best style, but there may be circumstances when a different approach may be preferable.

The influences on and effectiveness of different styles of management and leadership

Different leaders adopt different styles of management and leadership, but what determines the style adopted? There are a number of influences on this:

- The personality traits of the individual will have a bearing — some people feel they must always be in control and they will therefore be more autocratic in nature; others are more prepared to discuss things and lean towards a more democratic style.
- The type of business may have a bearing on the style adopted — the technology industry, which requires a high degree of creativity and innovation, may adopt a more laissez-faire style; the oil industry, where safety is paramount, may have a more bureaucratic style.
- The circumstances in which the business finds itself may determine the style adopted — when faced by difficult conditions, a more autocratic style may be adopted; in good times a more democratic style may be possible.

The effectiveness of different styles of leadership may be summed up in Table 1. It should also be noted that leadership style can be linked to and have a bearing on the business culture.

Knowledge check 14

Outline briefly the Tannenbaum Schmidt continuum and the Blake Mouton grid.

Business culture
The shared values, attitudes, standards and beliefs within a business.

Style	Advantages	Disadvantages
Autocratic	Effective for Theory X workers	May lose effectiveness over time
	Gives the leader control over decisions	Theory Y workers may not respond
	More effective when tasks are simple and repetitive	May lead to high levels of labour turnover and absenteeism
	Important when business facing problems	Does not develop future leaders
Democratic	Can result in high worker morale and motivation	The leader is not in total control of decision-making
	Motivates Theory Y workers	The leader has to abide by the views of others
Laissez faire	Results in high morale and motivation	If workers are insufficiently qualified, the whole business might suffer
	May develop future leaders	

Table 1 The advantages and disadvantages of different styles of leadership

Opportunities for analysis

- Analysis of the reasons for a particular style of leadership being adopted.
- Analysis of the benefits of a particular style of leadership.
- Analysis of the drawbacks of a particular style of leadership.

Opportunities for evaluation

- Evaluation of the usefulness of the Tannenbaum Schmidt continuum or the Blake Mouton grid.
- The extent to which one style of leadership (autocratic, democratic or laissez faire) is the most effective in a given situation.

Understanding management decision-making

The value of decision-making based on data (scientific decision-making) and on intuition

One key function of a leader is to make decisions, but decisions involve *risk* and *uncertainty*: get it right and the rewards can be high; get it wrong and it can lead to disaster. In any business, finance is limited and therefore with any decision there will be an **opportunity cost**. This means that by doing one thing the business will be unable to do something else, for example it might have the finance available for a new marketing campaign or a move into a new market, but not both. The option the business does *not* choose represents the opportunity cost. Management wherever possible will wish to reduce any risk in decision-making and to help there are various analytical tools that can be used in a scientific decision-making process.

Opportunity cost The cost of a foregone alternative. Where there is a choice, the opportunity cost is the decision the business did *not* make.

The use and value of decision trees in decision-making

Decision trees are an example of an analytical tool. They are tree-like diagrams used in determining the optimum course of action in situations where there are a number of possible alternatives with uncertain outcomes. The resultant diagram looks rather like a cluster of tree branches.

Constructing a simple decision tree

In order to construct a decision tree, it is necessary to have the following information:

■ the choice of decisions to be made and their cost
■ the probability of success for each decision
■ the payoff or financial outcome for each probability

All decision trees start with a square or decision node. The business might have an objective of increasing sales and be considering either:

■ a revitalised marketing campaign costing £2m, *or*
■ entering a new overseas market costing £3m

These two options are represented by forks coming from the decision node.

The business can now assess the probabilities of success and failure of each decision and these can be represented on the diagram as circles or chances nodes. Based on past experience of marketing campaigns and entering new markets, management can estimate the chances of success or failure and their likely financial outcomes.

For example, a revitalised marketing campaign may have a relatively high chance of success 75% (0.75) and therefore a 25% (0.25) chance of failure, leading to an expected payoff of £15m if successful and only £2.5m in the case of failure. Entering a new market, on the other hand, has only a 60% (0.6) chance of success and a 40% (0.4) chance of failure, but the expected payoff is likely to be £30m if successful and only £2m if a failure. It should be noted that the probability of success or failure should add up to 1 in each case (in this case, 0.75 + 0.25 = 1 and 0.6 + 0.4 = 1). All this can be represented in the diagram, together with the financial outcome of each probability, as shown in Figure 3.

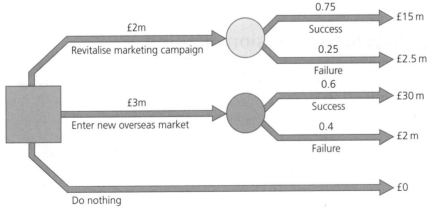

Figure 3 A simple decision tree

> **Decision trees** Tree-like diagrams used to determine the optimum course of action in situations where there are several possible alternatives with uncertain outcomes.

> **Exam tip**
>
> In any decision tree there is always the option to do nothing, which will have no cost or financial outcome.

We are now in a position to calculate the likely outcomes. To do this, multiply the payoff by the probability of success or failure, add them together and subtract the initial investment. This results in the overall potential payoff. Using the example above:

Revitalise marketing campaign $= (15 \times 0.75) + (2.5 \times 0.25) - 2$

$$= 11.25 + 0.625 - 2$$

$$= 11.875 - 2$$

$$= £9.875m$$

Enter new overseas market $= (30 \times 0.6) + (2 \times 0.4) - 3$

$$= 18 + 0.8 - 3$$

$$= 18.8 - 3$$

$$= £15.8m$$

In this example, entering a new overseas market appears to be the better option.

Decision trees can be a useful analytical tool in making a decision. They can help reduce risk, but they do have limitations. For example, the probabilities may be inaccurate as past experience is not necessarily an indicator of future outcomes. In addition, the probabilities may be influenced by a manager's own bias toward a particular outcome. However, they do provide a quantified outcome and when used with other quantitative (for example, net present value) and qualitative (for example, business objectives, external environment) information, decision trees can be a useful tool.

Sometimes a leader might ignore the scientific analysis when making decisions and use their intuition or 'gut feeling'. In some cases, particularly new innovative products it is very difficult to forecast consumer reaction and a leader has to be led by their gut feeling. In fact in a 2014 Economist Intelligence Unit study nine out of ten executives studies said if available data contradicted their intuition they would re-analyse it, ignore it or collect more information.

> **Knowledge check 15**
>
> Identify three key items of information needed in order to construct a decision tree.

Exam tip

Scientific decision-making is the systematic approach to collecting facts and applying logical decision-making techniques instead of generalising, trial and error or guessing, and this technique can be useful when trying to justify one decision over another. It never provides a complete answer, but it could give weight to a particular argument when making a judgement.

Influences on decision-making

Mission and objectives

To some extent, a business is guided in its decision-making by its mission and objectives. For example, decision-making in the Body Shop is influenced by its policy not to sell products tested on animals.

Ethics

Ethics is about making decisions that are morally correct and, in the last few years, it has assumed a much greater importance in decision-making. This can be seen in the growth of fair-trade products. However, when faced with a choice between profit and ethics, profit will invariably win. This is illustrated by Primark: despite being exposed as using sweatshops in developing countries, this clothing retailer still continues to prosper and make a profit.

Knowledge check 16

What do you understand by the term 'scientific decision-making'?

The external environment

Businesses operate within a dynamic external environment that is constantly changing. Interest rates, inflation and exchange rates all have an impact on decisions made, as well as technological developments, demographic changes and changes in taste and fashion. One example is the increasing popularity of online trading where some businesses such as Amazon have profited but others such as HMV have struggled. Another example is the move to digital photography, leading to the collapse of Kodak — once a giant in the photographic industry.

Competition

Businesses operate within a competitive environment and the intensity of the competition influences decision-making. The supermarket industry faces huge competition, not just between the 'big four' (Tesco, Sainsbury, Asda and Morrisons) but also between supermarket discounters Aldi and Lidl.

Resource constraints

When making decisions, a business needs to do so within the limits of its resources. Does it have the capital to finance a particular decision? Does it employ sufficient labour? Does it have the capacity to achieve higher production or sales? Has it recruited the right management talent?

Opportunities for analysis

- Analysis of either the benefits or drawbacks of using decision trees.

Opportunities for evaluation

- The extent to which decision trees might be effective in decision-making.
- Whether intuition is more reliable than data analysis in decision-making.
- The relative importance of the various influences on decision-making.

Understanding the role and importance of stakeholders

The need to consider stakeholder needs when making decisions

A stakeholder is an individual or group who has an interest in a business and includes consumers, employees, shareholders, suppliers, the local community and national government. Each stakeholder has different interests and it is important that these interests are recognised by management when making decisions, as shown in Table 2.

Stakeholder	Interests
Consumers	Quality, value for money
Employees	Job security, financial reward
Shareholders	Capital growth, income
Suppliers	Payment, security of orders
Local community	Ethics, social responsibility
National government	Taxation, employment

Table 2 Examples of stakeholder interests

Stakeholder needs and the possible overlap and conflict of these needs

As shown in Table 2, different stakeholders have different objectives. This could lead to potential conflicts of interest and it is important that such conflicts are recognised, balanced and managed by management.

Conflict arises when the needs of some stakeholder groups compromise the expectations of others. A business has to make choices; for example, in order to keep prices down for consumers it may look for cheaper suppliers, but in so doing this should *not* compromise their social and ethical standards (sweatshops, child labour).

Decisions made by a business may not bring immediate financial returns and require patience on the part of some stakeholders, particularly shareholders. Other decisions may add to the costs of a business such as efforts made to reduce carbon emissions — pleasing environmentalists but maybe not shareholders.

Investing in employees in terms of training and working conditions might seem to some as pandering to the workforce, but a business has to balance the effects of not investing in training and improving conditions with the costs and likely returns in terms of motivation and associated improvements in productivity and quality.

Although there are likely to be conflicts, there are also benefits to a stakeholder approach in terms of the reputation of a business and perhaps the quality of the products or service it provides. This may become more apparent in the long term rather than the short term.

Knowledge check 17

List six different stakeholder groups.

Exam tip

Looking at a decision in terms of short-term and long-term consequences can provide good judgement in answers when fully supported by evidence.

Stakeholder mapping

Stakeholder mapping is a map or visual representation of the various stakeholders of a business, showing their interest and importance to the business. A stakeholder map can be represented in a number of ways such as a chart with each stakeholder group categorised according to the level of interest and power it exerts over the company.

A stakeholder map can also be shown as a table similar to Table 3. In this example, the business is considering the extension of its present production facility by expanding into adjacent land that has become available. Stakeholder mapping helps in analysing the impact of this decision.

Stakeholder mapping
A visual tool used in strategy and stakeholder analysis to clarify and categorise various stakeholders according to the interest and power they have in a company.

Stakeholder	Type	Interest	Impact
Stakeholder 1	Employees	Jobs and job security	Likely to favour the decision
Stakeholder 2	Shareholders	Cost and long-term benefits	May need persuading depending on the current position of the business
Stakeholder 3	Local community	Jobs	Likely to be supportive, but those living close by may be less so
Stakeholder 4	Local council	Planning and changes to infrastructure	Depends on planning guidelines and the extent of changes to infrastructure required
Stakeholder 5	Environmentalists	Potential environmental impact	Could have a big impact if there are potential environmental issues

Table 3 Stakeholder mapping in the form of a table

What management are interested in are those stakeholders with the most influence and impact on the business. Mapping allows management to identify potential opportunities and threats to project implementation. As a result, appropriate strategies can be developed in order to minimise opposition and increase the likelihood of the success of a project.

It is also possible to undertake stakeholder mapping in the form of a matrix according to stakeholder interests and influences and whether they are high or low. As a result, those with both high interest and high influence have the most impact on a business and those with low interest and low influence have the least impact.

Knowledge check 18

How might stakeholder mapping help in the decision-making process?

Influences on and how to manage the relationship with different stakeholders

There are a number of influences on the relationship with stakeholders, one of which is illustrated by stakeholder mapping which is the likely impact of a stakeholder group on a decision. The greater the impact, the greater the influence and importance the business attaches to that stakeholder group. Other influences include the attitude of the board, financial pressure and conflict:

- Attitude of the board — it could be argued that some businesses place greater emphasis on profit than satisfying stakeholders such as those that use sweatshops.

- Financial pressure — this often results in businesses focusing on business survival rather than individual stakeholder groups, particularly those related to the environment.
- Conflict — this can and does often occur between individual stakeholder groups and it is important that a business manages the relationship with stakeholders in order to reduce the possibility of conflict.

The key to management is, first, to recognise the importance and influence of the various stakeholder groups as any underestimation of a particular group and its impact could lead to serious consequences. Secondly, and crucially, is the need for communication and consultation throughout the decision-making process. If stakeholders feel involved in the process, there is a greater chance for success. The importance of communication should not be underestimated; it will not guarantee success, but it will make it more likely. If decisions are approached in the right way, potential conflict can be significantly reduced.

Opportunities for analysis

- Analysis of the benefits of using stakeholder mapping.
- Analysis of the factors that might influence the importance of a particular stakeholder group.

Opportunities for evaluation

- The extent to which conflict between different stakeholder groups is inevitable.
- Evaluation of the relative importance of different stakeholder groups.

Summary

- The role of managers includes setting objectives, analysing, making decisions, reviewing and leading.
- Leadership styles include autocratic, democratic and laissez faire.
- Management and leadership styles can be represented on the Tannenbaum Schmidt continuum and the Blake Mouton grid.
- The style of leadership adopted depends on the circumstances, characteristics of the individual leader and the type of business.
- Opportunity cost is the cost of the next best alternative foregone.
- Business leaders wish to reduce risk and uncertainty in decision-making and for this reason they use scientific decision-making. This involves the use of analytical tools such as decision trees.

- A decision tree is a tree-like diagram used in determining the optimum course of action where there are a number of possible alternatives.
- Although decision trees can be useful, the calculation of probabilities is difficult and can be open to bias on the part of the decision-maker.
- Business leaders therefore sometimes ignore scientific analysis and go with their intuition or 'gut feeling' in making a decision.
- Stakeholders are any individual or group of individuals who have an interest in a business ranging from employees and shareholders to the local community and government.
- Different stakeholder groups have different interests and objectives and as a result there is potential for a conflict of interest between the different groups.
- Stakeholder mapping is a useful tool in trying to manage any potential conflicts.

■ Decision-making to improve marketing performance

The Chartered Institute of Marketing defines marketing as 'the process responsible for identifying, anticipating and satisfying customer requirements profitably'. This definition summarises the purposes of marketing, which are to:

- *Anticipate customers' requirements*. The first stage of marketing is to conduct market research in order to discover what customers want.
- *Satisfy those requirements in a way that delights customers*. The approach used by organisations to achieve this aim is known as the *marketing mix* (the 7Ps). The organisation plans a suitable *product*, charge an attractive *price*, put the product into the right location or *place* and uses *promotion* to make customers aware of the product. At the same time, it also pays attention to the *process* and *people* involved, as well as the *physical environment*.
- *Meet the needs of the organisation*. Marketing is intended to enable a business to meet its aims and objectives, such as making a profit.

Setting marketing objectives

The value of setting marketing objectives

Each functional area of a business has its own objectives or targets that contribute to achieving the overall corporate objectives. The marketing function might have one or more of the following objectives:

- *Increase sales (volume/value)*. Sales may be measured by the number of sales (volume) or the value of sales (£).
- *Increase in market share*. Market share is the number of sales achieved by one business compared to the total market and is calculated as a percentage.
- *Market size*. Businesses may also look to grow the overall market by, for example, appealing to a wider demographic, lowering prices or increasing advertising.
- *Introduce new product*. New product development may be an objective of the marketing department.
- *Increase customer retention and satisfaction*. Achieving sales is one thing; retaining customers is another. Businesses want to achieve this as with it comes **brand loyalty**, repeat purchases and word-of-mouth promotion.

Marketing objectives should be a part of the corporate business objectives and sit within the overall business plan and strategy. The value of setting marketing objectives include:

- target-setting — the business sets targets to aim for to ensure that marketing actions are focused instead of used inefficiently
- direction — this gives the business and staff a sense of working towards the same goals
- motivation — marketing objectives may be motivating, particularly if there are rewards associated with successful completion
- evaluation — marketing objectives provide evidence when it comes to evaluating the success of a particular marketing strategy

Brand loyalty When consumers become committed to a particular brand and make repeat purchases over time.

Knowledge check 19

Distinguish between sales value and sales volume.

External and internal influences on marketing objectives and decisions

There are a number of influences on marketing objectives, from both internally (within the business) and externally (outside of the business).

Internal influences on marketing objectives

- *Finance available*. The marketing department has to operate within the budget allocated and it is important to remember it will be competing with other departments when it comes to the allocation of budgets.
- *Expertise of personnel*. Success in terms of achieving objectives is in part dependent on the skills and expertise of departmental members.
- *Production capacity*. The objectives must be within the capabilities of a business, for example an increase of sales by 5% must be possible in terms of spare production capacity available.

External influences on marketing objectives

- *Competition*. When setting objectives, a business must be aware that other businesses in the same market will have their own set of targets and objectives that may seriously impact on its success.
- *Social attitudes*. Over time social attitudes may change, which might impact on the successful achievement of marketing objectives such as the greater awareness of fair trade within the chocolate market.
- *Economic factors*. Changes in the state of the economy may have an impact on the business, such as the sudden move into recession in 2008.
- *Legal/political factors*. Changes in government or the law can have an impact on marketing such as the ban on tobacco advertising.
- *Technological factors*. An example here would be the move toward **e-commerce**, which has had a big impact on many businesses — those achieving first-mover advantage in the grocery industry have gained market share over those that have been slow to incorporate e-commerce.

Opportunities for analysis

- Analysis of the benefits of setting marketing objectives.
- Analysis could revolve around the benefits of having a recognisable brand.
- Internal and external influences provide opportunities for analysis in terms of how they might impact on a business.

Opportunities for evaluation

- Evaluation of the value of setting an individual marketing objective or marketing objectives in general.
- The extent to which external constraints have more impact than internal influences.
- The extent to which a particular external constraint prevents a business achieving its objectives.

E-commerce The selling of goods and services through electronic means such as the internet.

Knowledge check 20

Using examples, distinguish between internal and external influences on marketing.

Exam tip

Although external factors are out of the control of the business, it is still possible to anticipate some changes and be prepared for them such as a change of government or an increase in interest rates.

Understanding markets and customers

The value of primary and secondary marketing research

There are a number of key calculations related to the market that you should be able to undertake if you are given certain information.

- Given total sales for a market and the sales for an individual firm, it is possible to calculate *market share*:

$$\text{Market share} = \frac{\text{sales (revenue) of individual firm}}{\text{total market sales}} \times 100$$

- Given an individual firm's sales for two different years, it is possible to calculate *sales growth*:

$$\text{Sales growth} = \frac{\text{current sales figure} - \text{previous sales figure}}{\text{previous sales figure}} \times 100$$

- Given market size for two different years, it is possible to calculate *market growth*:

$$\text{Market growth} = \frac{\text{current market size} - \text{previous market size}}{\text{previous market size}} \times 100$$

- Given the sales of an individual firm and its market share, it is possible to calculate *total market size*:

$$\text{Total market size} = \frac{\text{sales (revenue) of individual firm}}{\text{market share}} \times 100$$

Accurate and thorough information is essential to business success and the process of gathering, analysing and interpreting information about a market, product or service and its customers is known as **market research**. This takes the form of either primary or secondary research, and the data gathered may be either qualitative or quantitative.

Primary (field) research

Primary research is new research collected directly by or for a business in order to answer specific issues or questions. Examples include questionnaires, surveys and interviews with individuals or groups of people. The big advantage of primary research is that it can be tailored specifically to the needs of the business, but the downside is that it can be expensive to collect.

Secondary (desk) research

Secondary research makes use of information that has already been collected. Examples include published research reports, census information, newspaper reports and searching the internet. The benefit of secondary research is that it is low cost and relatively easy to collect, but it suffers from not being tailored to the specific needs of the business.

Knowledge check 21

What do you understand by the term 'market share'?

Market research The process of gathering, analysing and interpreting information about a market, product or service to be offered for sale in that market, and about the past, present and potential customers for that product or service.

Qualitative data

Qualitative data is based on opinion and is gathered by focus groups and face-to-face interviews to find out not just what people think about your product or service but also why they think it. It can be categorised but cannot be measured. Qualitative research can tell you:

- what people, customers and prospective customers think about your product or service
- how customers choose between different products
- the type of marketing message that has the most impact
- how price might affect decisions
- opinions about branding design and packaging

Quantitative data

Quantitative data is collected by asking people specific questions in a structured way using surveys and questionnaires so that you can produce hard facts and statistics to help guide marketing decisions. Quantitative research can provide a business with:

- data that can be represented in easy-to-read charts and graphs
- the means of establishing consumer profiles
- the ability to measure customer awareness
- the ability to determine market size

The most important feature of both qualitative and quantitative market research is that it helps to *reduce risk* for a business as it gives an indication about whether a certain product, service or strategy is likely to be successful and can therefore save money for the business.

Market mapping

Market mapping is a research method that identifies key customer requirements in a market and how existing products are positioned in that market. This can then be plotted on a map or grid that might enable a business to identify potential gaps in the market. Figure 4 (page 30) shows a market map for the supermarket industry where the supermarkets are placed according to price (low or high) and quality (low or high). As a result of market mapping, a business might try to reposition itself in order to achieve greater sales (market share). Are any of the supermarkets trying to re-position themselves as a result of the growing threat from Lidl and Aldi?

The value of sampling

When conducting primary market research, it is impossible to get the views and opinions of all your customers or prospective customers, so in order to overcome this problem the business interviews a sample of customers. In effect, the business studies a small group of people who are representative of a larger group. If this is done correctly, conclusions can be drawn from the sample and applied to the whole group. The benefit of sampling is that it is a cost-effective method of carrying out market research. It is, however, important that any sample selected is representative of the target consumer group and that the sample size is large enough.

Consumer profiles
Methods of describing consumers so that they can be grouped for marketing and advertising purposes. This might be according to age, sex, income, education level, occupation etc.

Knowledge check 22

Distinguish between qualitative and quantitative market research information.

Exam tip

Market mapping does not only plot geographical gaps in the market; it can also be used to spot product or service gaps.

Figure 4 Market mapping: the supermarket industry

Knowledge check 23

Briefly explain the importance of sampling in market research.

The interpretation of marketing data

Positive and negative correlation

After marketing information has been collected, it is then necessary to interpret the findings and draw conclusions. One method of interpretation is correlation: the extent to which there is a linear relationship between two variables. A business might wish to know whether it is worth spending more money on advertising and could look to see if in the past there had been a positive correlation between increased spending on advertising and increased sales. If there was a positive link, there could be a causal relationship. However, it is important to understand that the relationship may not always be positive; it could, in fact, be negative. Even if there is a positive relationship, this may not mean that it will *always* be the case and there will always be a limit in terms of the amount spent and the positive correlation. Figure 5 illustrates positive correlation, negative correlation and where there is considered to be no correlation.

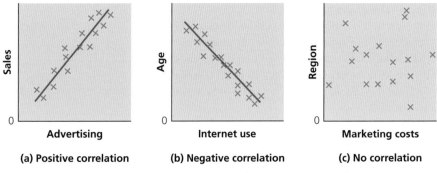

(a) Positive correlation **(b) Negative correlation** **(c) No correlation**

Figure 5 Positive correlation, negative correlation and no correlation

Knowledge check 24

What do you understand by the term 'correlation'?

Confidence intervals

In market research no estimate can be 100% reliable, so a business might like to know how confident it can be given a particular estimate. An important tool for dealing with this problem is that of confidence intervals, which helps a business to evaluate the reliability of an estimate. This is the margin of error that a researcher would experience if he or she asked a particular question to a sample group and expected to get the same answer back. For example, if a researcher used a confidence interval of 5 and 65% of respondents gave a particular answer, he could be sure that between 60% and 70% of the whole population would give the same answer.

When a researcher gives a confidence level, it is an expression of how confident that researcher is in the data collected. The most commonly used confidence level is 95%. This means that market researchers believe that their prediction will be correct 95% of the time. Therefore, using the example above, this market researcher would believe that 95% of the time between 60% and 70% of the population would give a particular answer.

- Sample size — the larger the sample, the greater the reliability. A wide confidence interval might indicate a small sample size although the relationship between the two is not linear.
- Frequency of response — the greater the number who gave a particular response, the greater the reliability.

Extrapolation

Forecasting is important to businesses because if they can accurately forecast future sales this enables them to reduce waste. If the business gets it wrong, however, it could end up with excess stock or insufficient stock for demand. One way of forecasting sales is through extrapolation, which uses known data to project future data, for example known sales figures to project future sales. This is shown in Figure 6.

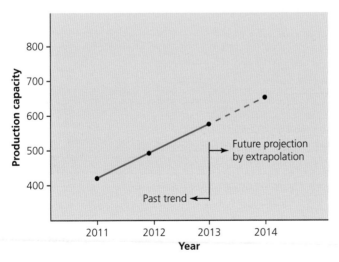

Figure 6 Extrapolation

Exam tip

Don't get confused by confidence level and confidence interval. Market researchers like to have a certain level of confidence in their result, e.g. 95%. The confidence interval is simply the margin of error above or below a result, e.g. +/–5%.

The value of technology in gathering and analysing data for marketing decision-making

Technology offers improved efficiency in marketing tasks and decision-making processes because of its ability to manage large volumes of data at much greater speed. For example, large amounts of information can be collected, stored, analysed and used to make marketing decisions with the Tesco loyalty card:

- It can provide better and faster communication with customers.
- It makes forecasting and extrapolation easier.
- It enables specific targeting of sales messages.
- Manufacturing can be linked to point of sale (POS) to respond to changing demand.

The change to IT-driven direct marketing and a reliance on technology may eclipse intuition. However, sometimes a manager's 'gut feeling' may be more effective in making key marketing decisions, particularly when circumstances are changing rapidly in the external environment. (See p. 12 for more information on the external environment.)

The interpretation of price and income elasticity of demand

Elasticity measures the likely change in demand for a product or service in response to a change in a variable such as income or price.

Price elasticity of demand (*PED*) measures how a change in the price of a good or service affects the demand for that good or service.

$$PED = \frac{\text{percentage change in demand for good A}}{\text{percentage change in price for good A}}$$

Income elasticity of demand (*YED*) measures how a change in a consumer's income affects the demand for a good or service.

$$YED = \frac{\text{percentage change in demand for a good}}{\text{percentage change in real income}}$$

If the change in price or income leads to a greater percentage change in the quantity demanded (ignoring the minus sign), then the calculation yields an answer greater than 1. This is *elastic demand*.

If the change in price or income leads to a smaller percentage change in the quantity demanded, then the calculation yields an answer less than 1. This is *inelastic demand*.

Price elasticity of demand The responsiveness of demand for a good or service to a change in its price.

Income elasticity of demand The responsiveness of demand for a good or service to a change in income.

Exam tip

When analysing elasticity, you should be interested only in whether the result is greater than 1 (elastic) or less than 1 (inelastic). *In other words, ignore the minus sign.*

Exam tip

For the exam, it is *not* necessary to know how to calculate price or income elasticity of demand, but you do need to understand the significance of the result. For example, what is the significance of a price elasticity of demand of −0.3 in comparison to one of −2.2?

A knowledge of elasticity is useful for a business as not all goods and services react in the same way to a change in price or income. Some such as bread and fuel are relatively inelastic in that a change in price or income is unlikely to result in any great change in demand, whereas luxury items are likely to have an elastic demand to changes in price or income. Therefore, if the price of an inelastic product or service is increased, demand is not greatly affected but revenue rises. If price is reduced, demand again will be minimally affected but revenue declines. With an elastic product or service, a rise in price leads to a fall in demand and revenue but a reduction in price leads to a rise in demand and revenue.

The same analysis can be made for income elasticity: a rise or fall in income has little impact on the demand and revenue received for inelastic goods but a more significant impact on elastic good. A rise in income leads to a rise in demand and revenue for income elastic goods and a fall in demand and revenue when income falls.

The value of the concepts of price and income elasticity of demand to marketing decision-makers

The calculation of elasticity can be a useful tool for a business when making marketing decisions, but it is just one factor in any decision. A pricing decision is not based on elasticity alone as other factors need to be taken into consideration such as the availability of substitutes, likely competitor actions, habit and brand loyalty. Income elasticity can be used by a business in trying to determine likely changes in the level of demand for its product or service in response to changes in income, but again this is influenced by competitor actions, habit, necessity, availability of substitutes etc.

The use of data in marketing decision-making and planning

The reason businesses collect large amounts of market research data is to help managers better understand the environment in which they operate and so improve the quality of decision-making. Data enables a business to establish consumer profiles providing facts, opinions and motivational information about the consumer. This can be the starting point for market planning and decision-making and help to reduce risk and uncertainty.

Knowledge check 25

How does a rise in price affect a business selling goods or services that are elastic in demand?

Opportunities for analysis

- Analysis in this area might be in general terms of the benefits of market research for a particular business or specifically regarding one aspect of this section of the specification, for example an analysis of how an understanding of price or income elasticity might help in decision-making.
- The importance of qualitative or quantitative data to a particular decision.
- The benefits or drawbacks of correlation and extrapolation in relation to a decision.

Opportunities for evaluation

- Any evaluation needs to be made in the context of the business in question and could relate to the value of research data in general or specific aspects of it.
- The value of a knowledge of elasticity in decision-making.
- The value of the particular sample used by a business.
- An evaluation of the different aspects of research undertaken by a business.

Making marketing decisions: segmentation, targeting, positioning

The process and value of segmentation, targeting and positioning

Market segmentation is the process of sub-dividing the market into clearly identifiable segments with similar wants or demand characteristics. The market can be segmented in a number of ways: age and sex are probably the most obvious, but it can also be divided by income, demographics or geographical differences.

The *target market* is the consumers that a business wishes to sell its products to and to whom therefore its marketing efforts are directed.

A clear link can be established between segmentation and targeting: having segmented a market, the business can more clearly define its target market. This provides the business with a number of benefits:

- Marketing can be aimed specifically at potential customers using relevant media and promotions to that target group.
- This more focused approach results in a more efficient use of resources, particularly finance.

However, there are a number of drawbacks, including:

- A business may ignore a particular group of potential consumers.
- It may fail to recognise and capitalise on changing tastes and trends among consumers.

Related to segmentation and target market is that of **market positioning**. This is where the marketing department creates an image for a particular product based on its target audience. This helps to establish a positive identity for the product or service within the eyes of the consumer and potential consumers who will buy their product rather than others on the market. This is created by the overall marketing strategy using the marketing mix. Market positioning can be illustrated in the supermarket industry, with Waitrose positioned at the top end of the market and Aldi and Lidl at the lower end.

Market positioning
This defines where a business's product or service stands in relation to other firms offering similar products and services in the market place, as well as in the mind of the consumer.

Influences on choosing a target market and positioning

Should the firm aim its product at a particular market segment (*niche marketing*) or at the whole market (*mass marketing*)? Both niche and mass marketing strategies can meet most of an organisation's marketing objectives. On the one hand, attracting a mass market can increase sales and therefore provide security. However, on the other hand, finding the right niche ensures market positioning and innovative products will be able to reach new segments, as shown in Figure 7.

Advantages of niche marketing	**Disadvantages of niche marketing**
• May be fewer competitors, as large companies are not attracted to a relatively small market • Small firms can compete more effectively because large firms will be less able to produce goods at low unit costs if demand is limited • Limited demand may suit a small firm that would lack the resources to produce on a large scale • A firm can adapt its product to meet the specific needs of the niche market, rather than compromise between the needs of many different groups of consumers • Can be easier for firms to target customers and promote their products effectively when they are selling only to a certain type of customer. The content of advertisements can be designed to appeal to the specific market segment being targeted	• The small scale of the market limits the chances of high profit • Small firms in niche markets can be vulnerable to changes in demand as they may have no alternative products to fall back on • An increase in popularity may attract larger, more efficient firms into the market
Advantages of mass marketing	**Disadvantages of mass marketing**
• Large-scale production is possible, which will help to lower costs per unit through factors such as bulk buying • The high number of customers enables companies to earn huge revenues • Allows firms to use the most expensive (and usually the most effective) marketing • Helps firms to fund the research and development tools needed to introduce new products • Increases brand awareness, which can help to sell a range of products	• High fixed capital costs are incurred, such as the purchase of large factories. This may prevent some firms from operating in this market • Firms in this market may be less flexible in the face of change such as a sudden reduction in popularity of a product • Can be difficult to appeal directly to each individual customer because mass-market products must be designed to suit all customers • Less scope for adding value. High-income customers may prefer high-priced, unique products

Figure 7 Niche versus mass marketing

Opportunities for analysis

■ Analysis might revolve around the benefits or drawbacks of segmentation, having a specific target market and positioning.

Opportunities for evaluation

■ Evaluation of the value of segmenting the market.
■ Evaluation of a particular position in the market.

Making marketing decisions: using the marketing mix

The elements of the marketing mix (7Ps)

The marketing mix is the combination of marketing activities that an organisation engages in in order to best meet the needs of its targeted market. Traditionally, the marketing mix was developed for fast-moving consumer goods and consisted of the four Ps: price, product, place and promotion. As the service sectors have become more aware of marketing, the mix has been developed to include people, process and the physical environment. Figure 8 illustrates the mix and the aspects involved with each of the seven Ps.

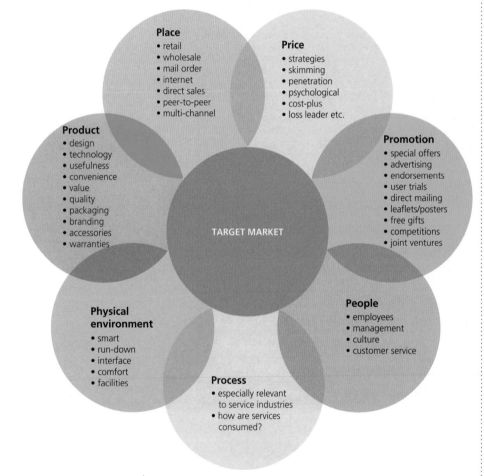

Figure 8 The 7Ps of marketing

When developing a marketing plan, a business should consider all aspects of the marketing mix as they are interlinked. For example, does pricing reflect the quality of the product? Does the choice of promotion reflect the distribution of goods?

The influences on and effects of changes in the elements of the marketing mix

The success of the marketing mix depends on ensuring that all the elements come together and are fully integrated. Many factors influence the elements of the mix. Examples include:

- *Market research results* may determine the price a business charges for its products or services and the places where these are sold.
- *Availability of finance* may influence the amount of money spent on promotion and product development.
- *New technology* may influence how often the product needs to be updated or whether it is made available for sale over the internet.
- *The type of product* may also have an influence — a convenience good will be marketed differently to a luxury product.

Not all marketing involves individual customers. Manufacturers buy raw materials from other companies. Retailers tend to buy their products directly from manufacturers. These activities are known as business-to-business (B2B) transactions. Persuading a business to buy products requires different approaches to those needed when targeting individual customers. This is known as business-to-business marketing — the main features of which are as follows:

- Transactions are much larger.
- Buyers and sellers have more specialist knowledge.
- The buyer's reputation often depends on the quality of the product purchased from the seller, so there may be more emphasis on this aspect.
- Promotions and advertisements tend to be more informative than persuasive, as buyers tend to base their decisions on factual information.
- Customer service is vital because poor service tends to become well known more quickly than in consumer marketing.

Product decisions

Product portfolio analysis

The aim here is to create a balance of products with widespread appeal. The Boston Matrix shown in Figure 9 is the usual way of showing this strategy.

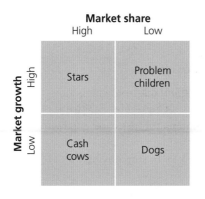

Figure 9 The Boston Matrix

Exam tip

Look for ways to integrate the different elements of the seven Ps. For the sake of convenience the seven Ps are taught as separate entities, but the marketing mix should be integrated. Where appropriate, look closely at the text in the exam to see how the different Ps need to work together. The mix is influenced by factors such as those given above, the market segment(s) being targeted and the actions of competitors.

Firms aim to produce products with a high market share ('cash cows' if market growth is low; 'stars' if the market is growing quickly). They need to think carefully about retaining products with a low market share ('dogs' or 'problem children'). Dogs, however, should not always be written off too lightly. Cadbury Whole Nut, for example, could be seen as a dog because it has only a 1% share of a low growth market (confectionery). However, this still represents almost £40 million in sales per year. Market mapping (see p. 29) can be used to investigate a product range to see if there are any market segments to which the product does not appeal and new products can be tailored to fit any gap that is discovered.

Knowledge check 26

What does the Boston Matrix show and what can it be used for?

Product life cycle

The product life cycle describes the various stages a product goes through from when it was first thought of through to its eventual decline. This concept can be linked to the Boston Matrix as a firm should aim to have as many products in growth and maturity as possible. Such products are the stars and cash cows. To achieve this in the long term, the firm needs to have a policy of new product development so that it always has products in the introduction and growth stages, ready to bring to maturity when required. Figure 10 illustrates this product life cycle.

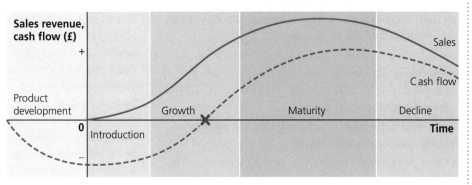

Figure 10 Stages in the product life cycle

In order to keep products in maturity — the most profitable stage of the product life cycle — *extension strategies* are used. Examples of extension strategies include:

- attracting new market segments
- increasing usage among existing customers
- modifying the product
- changing the image
- targeting new markets
- introducing new promotions, advertisements and price offers

The business also wants to make its product or service stand out from competitors as this will give it a competitive advantage. This might be achieved by establishing a *unique selling point (USP)*. If a firm can improve customer awareness and goodwill through making its product different from rival products, it can increase both its sales volume and price. As a result, customers are less likely to stop buying the firm's product.

Exam tip

Consider whether the product or service offered by the organisation in the scenario has a USP, or whether a USP could be developed by the organisation, and build this into the development of your answer.

New product development

Product is the central feature of the marketing mix. The key elements are:

- *Design of a product.* To the consumer this means reliability, safety, convenience of use and whether it is fashionable, aesthetic and durable. To the organisation, the key elements are whether the product satisfies consumer tastes, the financial viability, its effect on reputation and whether the company can produce it without difficulty.
- *New product development.* You need to know the stages involved in introducing a new product (from initial screening to the final launch), as well as linking new product development to the product life cycle, Boston Matrix, mind showering (also known as 'brainstorming'), market research and R&D (research and development). These are the sources of new product ideas. Organisations must be prepared to respond to the actions of competitors by developing new products and/or adapting existing products through the use of extension strategies. This ensures that they retain market share.

Factors influencing new product development include technology, competitors' actions and the entrepreneurial skills of managers and owners.

Technology

- New technology allows new products to be developed that are considered superior to existing products.
- Technology can lead to the development of totally new products.
- Production technology has advanced considerably, enabling organisations to produce goods and services that are more advanced and cheaper to produce.
- Businesses can more easily produce goods and services that are made to the individual specifications of the consumer.
- Technology is now allowing companies to be aware of consumer tastes.

Competitors' actions

- The introduction of a new product by a competitor may take away market share, forcing a business to respond.
- New products from competitors can give ideas for new products to a business.

Entrepreneurial skills of managers and owners

If an entrepreneur is the first to spot a gap in a market or think of a potentially successful idea, his or her business can gain first-mover advantage.

Pricing decisions

The factors that influence price are based on the forces of demand and supply. Demand factors include the nature of the product, consumers' incomes, competitors' products, tastes and fashion. Supply factors include costs of inputs (mainly raw materials and wages), technology, production methods and environmental conditions. The type of market is crucial too: the number of competitors influences a firm's pricing and its power to set prices depends on its market share.

When considering pricing decisions, it is useful to know the difference between *pricing strategies* and *pricing tactics*. There are overlaps between these classifications, but a simple distinction is outlined below.

Pricing strategies

Pricing strategies are adopted over the medium to long term to achieve marketing objectives. Such strategies include:

- skimming pricing — a high price is set to yield a high profit margin
- penetration pricing — low prices are set to break into a market
- price leaders — large companies that set market prices, which are then followed by price takers (smaller firms)
- price takers — small businesses that tend to follow the prices set by other firms (price leaders)

Pricing tactics

Pricing tactics are adopted in the short term to suit particular situations. Examples of such tactics are:

- loss leaders — very low prices that are used to encourage consumers to buy other, fully priced, products
- psychological pricing — prices that are set to give an impression of value (for example, £99 rather than £100)

Influences on pricing decisions

Firms need to consider their *costs* when setting price, as the eventual price must be high enough to allow a reasonable level of profit for the firm. For this reason, many firms use *cost-plus pricing*. This is where the firm calculates its unit costs and then adds on a *mark-up*. The mark-up allows for risk and helps the firm to make a profit by setting a price that exceeds costs. *Elasticity of demand* may also be considered when making pricing decisions.

Technology also has an influence on pricing as with e-commerce a business is able to change prices regularly. Airlines, hotels and many retailers can now adopt a flexible approach to pricing, offering some goods and services cheaply in order to attract consumers.

Decisions about the promotional mix

Promotion attempts to draw consumers' attention to a product, brand or company. It can be above-the-line or below-the-line:

- above-the-line — advertising through media, such as newspapers, television, radio, the cinema and posters
- below-the-line — all other types of promotion, such as public relations, branding, merchandising, sponsorship, direct marketing, personal selling and competitions

Advertising can be *informative* or *persuasive*. In general, advertising aims to raise awareness, publicise changes and new products and increase brand loyalty. Other promotions (except public relations and sponsorship) tend to be more targeted, trying to clinch the final purchase through special offers, persuasive selling or point-of-sale displays. Companies tend to plan advertising and promotions that support each other.

Knowledge check 27

With the use of examples, explain the difference between skimming pricing and penetration pricing.

The promotional mix

This consists of the various methods of promotion used in order to achieve overall marketing targets. A key element in this is *branding* — the process of differentiating a product or service from its competitors through the name, sign, symbol, design or slogan linked to that product. By establishing a recognisable brand, it creates a perception of a product or service that consumers trust and have confidence in, giving them a reason to choose a product or service over that of its competitors and enabling a business to increase sales. As a result, price may be more inelastic and it could be easier to launch new products under that brand name.

Other elements involved in the promotional mix are:

- public relations (PR) — this involves gaining favourable publicity through the media
- merchandising — attempts to persuade consumers to take action at the point of sale (POS), also known as the point of purchase (POP) — are known as merchandising. Examples include shop displays, sampling opportunities and special offers
- sales promotions — short-term incentives used to persuade consumers to purchase. Popular methods include competitions, free offers, coupons, three for the price of two promotions, BOGOF (buy one, get one free) offers, introductory offers, product placement (featuring a product in a film or television programme), credit terms and endorsements by famous personalities
- direct selling — this takes three main forms:
  - direct mail — promotions that are sent directly to the customer/person who has been targeted. Internet links are also used
  - telephone — many companies use telephone contact as it is easier to communicate directly with the customer
  - door-to-door drops — promotions that are delivered directly to houses. These are often delivered with the local free newspaper and can be cost effective and targeted
- personal selling — particularly important in commercial marketing, where a company's sales force contacts other firms that are seen as potential customers
- advertising — the main media used are:
  - television
  - radio
  - cinema
  - national and regional newspapers
  - posters
  - magazines
  - internet and other electronic media

When deciding what form of promotion to choose, a business considers the following factors:

- objectives of the campaign
- costs and budgets
- the target market
- legal factors
- customers' views

Knowledge check 28

What do you understand by the term 'promotional mix'?

Exam tip

Always read questions carefully as identifying the key focus of the question ensures your answer is fully focused. For example, when answering a question on the promotional mix, don't confuse it with the marketing mix.

Distribution (place) decisions

This involves getting products to the places where customers can buy them. Shops do not give space automatically to suppliers: many sales people are employed to persuade retailers to stock a product rather than trying to persuade customers to buy it. Customers cannot buy it if retailers do not sell it.

Traditionally, the method of getting a product from producer to customer was:

producer > wholesaler > retailer > consumer

Many companies now bypass the wholesaler. However, not only is the wholesaler often bypassed today, it has also become possible to bypass the retailer. The growth of the internet and e-commerce has had a significant impact on the way consumers do their shopping.

On the other hand, many businesses use multi-channel distribution: their products are available not only through retailers but also directly to the consumer using the internet, mail order or telephone.

Factors influencing the method of distribution include:
- type of product (for example, whether it is perishable)
- geography of the market (for example, whether it is scattered)
- complexity of the product (for example, whether it needs direct contact with the producer or an expert retailer)

Decisions relating to other elements of the marketing mix: people, process and physical environment

People

People are the most important element of any service or experience. First impressions are important and the person who picks up the telephone to any enquiry or serves the consumer in a shop or café can in an instant make or break a sale. The reputation of a business rests with the people involved with it and it is essential they are well trained and motivated. This relates predominantly to the area of customer service, but it can also be extended to other areas of the business.

Process

This involves how the products get to the customers and in the past customer experience has come under the function of operations. However, as customer experience can affect the success of marketing decisions, it has now become part of the marketing mix. Whether the service provided is efficient or not can have a big effect on the level of sales. This ranges from the functionality of websites to waiting time on the telephone and at checkout queues.

Physical environment

This relates to the actual environment of a shop or restaurant: where it is located and how it looks have a big impact on a consumer's decision to use it. It also relates to the ease of use of a website and how realistic the products look. Products are often shown from a variety of different angles and include previous customer reviews to encourage new customers to purchase.

Knowledge check 29

What do you understand by the term 'e-commerce'?

The importance of and influences on an integrated marketing mix

The marketing mix refers to all the ingredients of marketing (the 7Ps) and can be likened to the ingredients of a recipe. All the ingredients are necessary for the success of the recipe and they must be integrated in the right way, but subtle changes can be made to suit its appeal for different groups. This is the same with the marketing mix: all the ingredients are necessary and must be integrated, but it is possible to make subtle changes in the mix to change the appeal of the product or service or to respond to changing circumstances.

Possible influences on the marketing mix include:

- the position in the product life cycle — a product in the growth stage requires a different mix to a product in the maturity stage
- the Boston Matrix — a star requires a different mix to a cash cow
- the type of product — for example, if it is a necessity or a luxury
- the marketing — business to business (B2B) or business to consumer (B2C)
- the marketing objectives — changing objectives are likely to require changes to the mix
- the target market — the mix needs to be adjusted to best appeal to the target group
- competition — sometimes the mix may be changed in order to gain an advantage over competitors or in order to respond to a competitor's actions
- market conditions and positioning — whether the market in which the business is operating has perfect or monopolistic competition, or is an oligopoly or a monopoly as these all affect the way the mix is integrated

Understanding the value of digital marketing and e-commerce

Developments in technology have had a significant impact on business marketing function. The power of social media cannot be underestimated and from a business point of view it can have both positive and negative impacts. If a business can tap into this with its **digital marketing**, it can be a cost-effective way of boosting sales. However, on the downside a business reputation could be damaged quickly via social media.

In addition, greater contact is established between consumer and business, with the ability of customers to build their own products and write reviews of products or services purchased. Other benefits of digital marketing include the ability to gather more detailed information about consumers and to build relationships with them, for example how Amazon continuously recommends products based on a consumer's past shopping purchases. Digital marketing also makes it easy for any business to set up and sell almost anywhere in the world.

Knowledge check 30

Why have the 3Ps of people, process and physical environment become an important consideration in the marketing mix?

Knowledge check 31

Identify two ways in which the marketing mix might change as a product moves from growth to maturity in the product life cycle.

Digital marketing Marketing that makes use of electronic devices such as personal computers, smartphones, tablets and game consoles to engage with stakeholders.

Digital marketing can have great benefits for a business, but it can also have significant drawbacks. For example, there is little control over the customer reviews that can seriously harm a firm's reputation. Customers are also at the mercy of the internet where viruses and hackers can cause problems for both business and consumer.

Outline two benefits of using e-commerce.

Opportunities for analysis

- Opportunities for analysis are numerous here and might include consideration of the constraints that affect marketing objectives and strategy as well analysis of specific aspects of the mix.
- Considering the benefits of product portfolio analysis.
- Analysis of the benefits of a knowledge of product life cycle to a business.
- Analysis of the benefits of a USP to a business.
- Analysis of the circumstances in which a penetration or skimming pricing strategy might be adopted.
- Considering the benefits of an appropriate promotional mix.
- Analysis of the benefits or drawback of digital marketing to a particular business.
- Analysis of the reasons for people, process and physical environment being important.

Opportunities for evaluation

- Opportunities for evaluation are also numerous and may be undertaken in terms of the overall value of an integrated marketing mix or an evaluation of specific aspects of the mix.
- To what extent one aspect of the mix is the most important aspect for a particular business.
- Evaluation of influences on the mix.
- To what extent a business can afford to ignore e-commerce.
- Evaluation of the impact of market condition on the marketing mix.
- Evaluation involving recognising that other factors in addition to alterations in the marketing mix can affect competitiveness.

Summary

- The purpose of marketing is to anticipate and satisfy customers' needs while at the same time meeting the needs of the organisation in terms of, for example, making a profit.
- Marketing objectives include objectives related to sales, market size, market share, market and sales growth and brand loyalty.
- External influences on marketing decisions include competition, social factors, economic factors, legal and political factors and technological factors.
- Market research is the systematic gathering and interpretation of information related to a business's product or service.
- Market research may be in the form of quantitative or qualitative data and gathered from either primary or secondary sources.
- Sampling in market research is where information is gathered from a small group of respondents that is representative of the market as a whole.
- In interpreting marketing data, correlation is where relationships are determined between two variables.
- Extrapolation is the extension of a trend line to forecast future data.
- Elasticity of demand is a measure of the responsiveness of demand to changes in a variable, for example, price or income.
- Elastic demand (answers greater than 1) means that a price change leads to a larger percentage change in quantity, whereas inelastic demand (answers less than 1) means that a change in price leads to a smaller percentage change in the quantity demanded.
- Segmentation is the division of a market into sub-groups sharing the same characteristics such as age, sex or income.
- Niche marketing aims a product at a particular market segment, whereas mass marketing aims a product at the whole market.
- Niche marketing has fewer competitors and it may be easier to target customers and promote products, but the small scale of the market limits the chances of high profit and firms may be vulnerable to changes in demand.
- Mass marketing has lower costs and high customer numbers leading to high sales revenue. However, there is less flexibility.
- Business-to-business marketing usually involves large transactions, with promotions and advertising being informative rather than persuasive.
- The key elements of the marketing mix are the relationships between product, price, promotions, place, people, process and physical environment (the 7Ps).
- Product is a key element of the marketing mix and it depends heavily on design and new product development.
- A unique selling point (USP) adds value as it differentiates a product from others in the market.
- The Boston Matrix shows the relationship between market growth and market share.
- Extension strategies aim to extend the life of a product by modifying it, changing its image, attracting new segments or targeting new markets.
- Promotion can be above-the-line advertising by media or below-the-line through other promotions such as competitions.
- The promotional mix includes public relations, branding, merchandising, sales promotions, direct selling, personal selling and advertising.
- Pricing strategies include skimming, penetration, price leaders and price takers.
- Pricing tactics include loss leaders and psychological pricing.
- The place element of the marketing mix involves ensuring that products are available in places where customers can buy them.
- The 3Ps of people, process and physical environment, which were once more applicable to the service industry, have been added to the traditional four Ps of the marketing mix.
- A firm's competitiveness depends on employee skills and motivation, effectiveness of the marketing mix, financial planning and control, efficiency of operations and quality procedures, innovation and investment, and enterprise.

Questions & Answers

This section contains a variety of exam-style questions that you are likely to encounter. It includes multiple choice, short-answer, data response and case studies found on both AS and A-level papers, and essay questions that will only be found on A-level papers. There is also a section on quantitative skills question practice providing additional examples of the type of calculation questions you are likely to be faced with. The multiple-choice and short-answer questions aim to give a broad coverage of the content of this book, whereas the data-response questions are directed at a specific area of content. Finally, there are two essay questions in this section but do be aware that you will only find this style of question on the A-level papers.

For each short-answer, data-response and essay question you will find sample answers with exam advice. One of the sample answers will be a good response and the other a weaker answer, with the aim of illustrating common errors made by students and examples of good practice in the hope that you will, with practice, be able to develop your own skills.

Questions

As the multiple-choice and short-answer questions give a broad coverage of the content of this book, it would make sense to use these towards the end of your revision period in order to check your knowledge. However, the data-response questions could be used as you complete an area of content.

Sample answers

Resist the temptation to study the answers before you have attempted the questions. If you make a mistake here it is not the end of the world and practice at developing your own responses will help you to hone your skills. Once you have written your answer, look at the sample responses and identify the strengths and weaknesses of your own work. Using the Questions & Answers section in this way should result in the quality of your answers improving.

Assessment

AS and A-level papers do not just test how well you know the content of the subject. There is a clear set of skills that are tested and it is essential that you are aware of these and have some idea of how to satisfy them. The following skills are tested:

- *Knowledge and understanding.* This relates to the content of the specification and how well you know and understand the various business concepts, theories and ideas.
- *Application.* This focuses on your ability to relate your knowledge and understanding of the subject content to a particular situation or scenario (such as that in a particular case study).
- *Analysis.* This is the ability to develop an extended line of argument related to a particular question.
- *Evaluation.* This is making a judgement by weighing up the evidence provided.

It is important to understand that not all questions test all the skills set out above and as a result it is important that you are able to recognise which skills are being tested. The basis of all questions will be some element of knowledge, but what other skills will be required? The clue to this is in the question command words. Some commonly used ones are outlined below.

Application

The following command words require you to apply your answer to the context of the question or case:

- 'Explain...'
- 'Calculate...'

Analysis

The following command words require you to develop a relevant argument:

- 'Analyse...'
- 'Explain why...'
- 'Examine...'

Remember that your answer has to be in context (application).

Evaluation

The following command words require you to make a judgement:

- 'Evaluate...'
- 'Discuss...'
- 'To what extent...'
- 'Justify...'

Remember again that in an answer that requires evaluation your arguments must be developed (analysis) and they must also be in context (application).

It is worth remembering that most students who have studied Business seriously and who under-perform do not do so because of a lack of knowledge but because of a lack of good exam technique. If you understand the skills that are being tested, recognise how to develop them and are prepared to practise them, you will be one step ahead of the game.

Multiple-choice questions (AS and A-level)

Question 1

The benefits of setting business objectives include: (1 mark)

A They can be used to evaluate performance and help to identify a target market

B They can be used in formulating a mission statement and be motivational for key personnel

C They can help to identify a target market and be used in formulating a mission statement

D They can be used to evaluate performance and be motivational for key personnel

Question 2

In a period of economic recession, the most appropriate objective of a business might be: (1 mark)

A Growth

B Profit

C Survival

D Improved social responsibility

Question 3

Which of the following are both examples of variable costs? (1 mark)

A Directors' salaries and rent

B Direct labour and raw materials

C Rent and rates

D Raw materials and rates

Question 4

Which of the following most clearly defines revenue? (1 mark)

A Turnover – total costs

B Number of units sold × total costs

C Sales × total costs

D Price per unit × number of units sold

Question 5

The greatest benefit of incorporation for a business might be: (1 mark)

A Maintaining control of the business

B Limited liability

C Keeping affairs private

D Becoming a public corporation

Question 6

Which of the following best defines market capitalisation? (1 mark)

A The capital invested in a business

B The amount of capital invested in marketing

C Share price × number of shares issued

D The key market in which a business operates

Question 7

Scientific decision-making is best described as: (1 mark)

A   The use of experiments in decision-making

B   The reduction of risk in decision-making

C   The use of analytical tools in order to reduce risk in decision-making

D   The use of decision trees in order to reduce risk in decision-making

Question 8

A stakeholder is best defined as: (1 mark)

A   A shareholder

B   An individual or group who has an interest in a business

C   Anyone who has a personal investment in a business

D   An employee who has a personal stake in a business

Question 9

From the following information, which answer correctly calculates Company X's market share? (1 mark)

   Total value of sales in market = £23.5m

   Company X's sales = £2.25m

A   1044.44%   C   9.57

B   957%   D   9.57%

Question 10

Income elasticity of demand refers to: (1 mark)

A   The responsiveness of demand to a change in a variable

B   How demand changes in response to a change in price

C   The responsiveness of income to a change in demand

D   The responsiveness of demand to a change in income

Question 11

A niche market is: (1 mark)

A   A nice market in which to operate

B   A market that has a large number of competitors

C   A small part of a much larger market

D   A market that sells a variety of niche products

Question 12

A cash cow on the Boston Matrix has: (1 mark)

A   High market share and low market growth

B   Low market share and high market growth

C   Low market share and low market growth

D   High market share and high market growth

Answers to multiple-choice questions

Question 1

Correct answer D.   (1 mark)

ⓔ With this type of question it is necessary to read the options carefully in order to avoid making a mistake. In this case, evaluating performance and being motivational for personnel are correct.

Question 2

Correct answer C.   (1 mark)

ⓔ In a period of recession businesses are likely to find it difficult to grow and make profit. There are also unlikely to be funds available for ethical issues. Survival is the correct answer.

Question 3

Correct answer B.   (1 mark)

ⓔ Take care reading the question as there are two possibilities in each option and both must be correct. Option B is the correct answer as both direct labour and raw materials vary with output.

Question 4

Correct answer D.   (1 mark)

ⓔ Multiple-choice questions highlight the need for good subject knowledge. If you have this, it is easy to spot the answer is price per unit × number of units sold.

Question 5

Correct answer B.   (1 mark)

ⓔ This should be a relatively straightforward question — limited liability is the greatest benefit.

Question 6

Correct answer C.   (1 mark)

ⓔ Market capitalisation is a measure of the value of a business, so the correct answer is share price × number of shares issued.

Question 7

Correct answer C. (1 mark)

ⓔ Care is needed with this question: scientific decision-making it is not just the reduction of risk, it is the use of analytical tools in reducing that risk.

Question 8

Correct answer B. (1 mark)

ⓔ All options might be stakeholders, but the correct definition is any individual or group who has an interest in a business, making B the correct answer.

Question 9

Correct answer D. (1 mark)

ⓔ Providing you know the correct formula and have remembered your calculator, this is an easy question.

$$\text{Market share} = \frac{\text{sales (revenue) Company X}}{\text{total market sales}} \times 100$$
$$= \frac{2.25}{23.5} \times 100$$
$$= 9.57\%$$

Question 10

Correct answer D. (1 mark)

ⓔ Note this question is about income elasticity, so it is the responsiveness of demand to a change in income.

Question 11

Correct answer C. (1 mark)

ⓔ A niche market is a small part of a much larger market.

Question 12

Correct answer A. (1 mark)

ⓔ This question illustrates the importance of sound knowledge of subject content. If you have this it is easy to recognise a cash cow as having a high market share and low market growth.

Short-answer questions (AS and A-level)

1   Explain one reason why a business sets objectives. (3 marks)

ⓔ This question requires one reason to be identified with a brief explanation of why it is important. One sentence is often adequate and time should not be wasted writing over-long answers.

> **Student A**
>
> By having specific objectives, a business is able to measure and evaluate its performance and as a result it can then revise its targets and develop new plans to achieve the revised goals.

ⓔ **3/3 marks awarded.** This answer gives a clear explanation for setting objectives.

> **Student B**
>
> Objectives can be motivating for those responsible for achieving them providing they are realistic. A benefit for the business is that they can be motivating and therefore lead to greater output.

ⓔ **1/3 marks awarded.** The explanation here is less convincing. Yes, objectives can be motivating, but probably only for those responsible for achieving the target, leading to greater job satisfaction and perhaps a greater commitment to the business. As a result, this answer might just get 1 mark for identifying a benefit.

2   Using the information below, calculate the total costs of the business. (4 marks)

Selling price	£5.00
Units sold	25,000
Variable cost per unit	£2.00
Fixed costs	£10,000

ⓔ This is a simple calculation, but remember that the variable cost given is per unit and so it needs to be multiplied by the number of units to achieve the total variable costs figure. Add this to the fixed costs and total cost is arrived at.

> **Student A**
>
> Total costs = fixed costs + variable costs
>
> 10,000 + (25,000 × 2) = £60,000

ⓔ **4/4 marks awarded.** This is the correct answer, scoring full marks.

> **Student B**
>
> Total costs = fixed costs + variable costs
>
> 10,000 + 2 = £10,002

ⓔ **3/4 marks awarded.** This student has not calculated the variable cost total, but this is just one error and everything else is correct.

3 **Explain how a rise in interest rates might affect a business selling luxury products.** (5 marks)

ⓔ To answer this question it is necessary to identify how a rise in interest rates will affect demand. This then needs to be explained in relation to a firm selling luxury goods.

Student A

A rise in interest rates is likely to mean that consumers have less in the way of disposable income because of higher interest payments on any borrowing. With less disposable income, consumers concentrate spending on necessities and a business selling luxury products is likely to see a decline in sales.

ⓔ **5/5 marks awarded.** This is a slightly short answer, but not only does it demonstrate understanding, it also applies this to a seller of luxury goods. This response is awarded full marks.

Student B

A change in interest rates has a number of implications for consumers. For those with mortgages or loans, they will have to pay out more in interest and therefore have less disposable income and others who have money saved will receive more in interest which might encourage them to save more. All of this could mean less spending in the economy.

ⓔ **2/5 marks awarded.** Clearly this student understands the impact of a rise in interest rates on consumers, but there has been no attempt to relate this to a seller of luxury goods and therefore the candidate has not really answered the question.

4 **Explain one benefit of market segmentation to a business.** (3 marks)

ⓔ This requires a brief explanation of one benefit only. Don't fall into the trap of writing over-long answers; one sentence is often enough.

Student A

If a business knows the specific segment of the market it is aiming its product or service at — such as age group or income — then it can direct its marketing specifically at that group, thereby saving money.

ⓔ **3/3 marks awarded.** A good answer — full marks.

Student B

Market segmentation is the division of a company's market into distinct groups such as different ages, income or sex.

ⓔ **1/3 marks awarded.** This answer gives a definition of segmentation only.

5 Explain why the product might be the most important aspect of a pharmaceutical business marketing mix.

(5 marks)

(e) The secret to this answer is knowing what a pharmaceutical business is. It emphasises the importance of wider reading in business and an awareness of various industries and examples of companies that operate in these industries.

Student A

For a pharmaceutical business, the product is everything. It is responsible for developing new drugs which take a great deal of time, investment and testing before they are put on the market. Usually the company has a patent on a new drug so it can charge a high price, the place it sells the drug is pre-determined (pharmacies) and if the drug is new and effective it needs little in the way of promotion. So for this type of business product is likely to be the most important aspect of the marketing mix.

(e) **5/5 marks awarded.** A clear answer, fully in context. Full marks.

Student B

For this type of business, the product is likely to be most important as it is the key to its success. Other factors might also be important and usually an integrated marketing mix is required. This links product, price, promotion, process and people together. This would be no different for a pharmaceutical firm where, although the product is key, it needs an integrated marketing mix.

(e) **2/5 marks awarded.** This student understands the marketing mix, but is probably unsure of what a pharmaceutical business produces and so there is no context in the answer.

6 Analyse the potential benefits to a large chocolate manufacturer of using market mapping.

(9 marks)

(e) The command word here is 'analyse' and therefore this response requires fully developed arguments related to the benefits of market mapping to a chocolate manufacturer. Don't consider any drawbacks and make sure your answer is fully focused on a chocolate manufacturer.

Student A

Market mapping in this case would involve the chocolate manufacturer plotting on a grid the various chocolate bars sold in the market. The grid could have price on the x-axis and quality on the y-axis. This would enable the business to see if there were any gaps in the market. For example, the map might reveal that currently there were few high quality, high price chocolate bars available. This might lead the business to undertake further research to see if consumers actually wanted this type of product. It might even develop a product, perhaps a spin-off from one of the existing high quality, high price products, into a chocolate bar to test on the market. Overall, this type of analysis market mapping could help reduce risk and save money for the business.

ⓔ 9/9 marks awarded. This is an excellent answer with a clear understanding of market mapping demonstrated in the first two sentences. There then follows a good chain of argument developing the potential benefit for a chocolate manufacturer (context) and as a result there is the potential to achieve full marks.

Student B

Market mapping is a tool used in market research that helps in business decision-making. Its particular benefit is that it helps reduce risk and therefore can save costs for a business. If a new business is setting up or an existing business is thinking of opening a new branch, it might undertake market mapping in order to identify existing competitors and place them on a map. This would enable the business to identify any potential gaps and therefore lead to the best location and giving the best chance of being successful.

ⓔ 4/9 marks awarded. This student understands market mapping and analyses a benefit, but there is no application (context) to the chocolate manufacturer. This is a common error made by students and it is a pity that this candidate might get only 4 marks for this response.

7 A business operating in a highly competitive market is considering reducing its prices. Analyse the possible benefits for the business if it goes ahead with this decision.

(9 marks)

ⓔ 'Analyse' means to provide a fully developed argument of the benefits of a price reduction in a competitive market. There is no need to consider the drawbacks.

Student A

A highly competitive market is one where there are lots of businesses all competing for market share. In such a market, demand is likely to be highly responsive to price — a small change in price is likely to lead to a much greater change in demand. In other words, the product or service is going to be price elastic. In theory, this means that a fall in price would lead to a rise in demand, creating greater revenue and profit. Providing competitors did not respond by also lowering prices, then not only would revenue increase but also market share. As such, this would be the benefit that a business would expect from a reduction in price. It would probably also help if it had something that made its product stand out, as this would give the consumer even more reason for buying its product.

ⓔ 8/9 marks awarded. This is a good answer where the student demonstrates a sound understanding of competitive markets and elasticity. This is linked to the ideas of increased revenue and market share, creating a good answer.

In a competitive market, a reduction in price is likely to lead to a rise in demand as consumers will always be looking for the cheapest prices. For example, the market for petrol is highly competitive and consumers are attracted to the cheapest seller. If a supermarket reduces its prices, consumers will go there and they will benefit from greater sales and profit.

This is all very well in theory, but in practice other supermarkets are also likely to reduce their prices so there will be no change in demand and just a fall in revenue and profit. This is why Tesco offers money off fuel linked to spending in the shop — the more you spend, the cheaper the fuel. The supermarket still benefits from the reduction in fuel price, but without competitors also reducing their price. On top of which they also achieve greater sales in the shop.

ⓔ **4/9 marks awarded.** The first paragraph is similar but less detailed than Student A and the second is addressing the drawbacks which are not required in this answer.

Data-response questions (AS and A-level)

Question 1 Time for Coffee

Joe and Gina had worked together for years and often talked of running their own business rather than working for someone else. With their children grown up and their local town becoming increasingly popular as a tourist and outdoor activity centre, the opportunity seems to be there. Recent projections indicate significant growth in numbers of visitors over the next 10 years, with plans already given the green light for improvements in infrastructure by the local authority. The town is growing and they feel there is a real gap in the market for a place where people can enjoy quality coffee in comfortable surroundings. If they can get in before any of the big chains, Joe and Gina could establish a reputation and gain first-mover advantage.

They looked at the mission statements of a number of the leading chains and, wanting to make their business stand out, they came up with the following: 'Time for Coffee: time to enjoy, time to relax in the comfort and knowledge we are here to provide a first-class service.'

Joe and Gina's overall objective is to be successful and to make a profit and their early projections seem to suggest this is possible. Table 1 gives the likely costs, spend and customer numbers over the first 3 years of existence.

	Year 1	Year 2	Year 3
Fixed costs	£40,000	£40,000	£40,000
Variable costs per customer	£2.00	£2.00	£2.00
Average spend per customer	£5.00	£5.00	£5.00
Number of customers	10,000	13,500	16,000

Table 1 Projections for costs, spend and customer numbers for Time for Coffee

Joe feels that given the development of the infrastructure and facilities planned and the expected growth in visitor numbers, their estimates are relatively conservative. He is optimistic that a profit might be achieved much earlier and that they would be able to grow and develop the business with new outlets in neighbouring towns. Gina is less convinced by the figures and feels that survival should be the most important objective over the first 3 years.

(a) Explain the importance of profit to Joe and Gina. (4 marks)

ⓔ 'Explain' means to show why profit is important. The key here is to make sure the answer is related specifically to Joe and Gina.

(b) Calculate the percentage change in profit between year 2 and year 3. (6 marks)

ⓔ This answer requires a number of numerical calculations: the profit for years 2 and 3, the change from year 2 to year 3 and finally that change as a percentage of year 2 profit.

(c) Explain how Joe and Gina's mission statement differs from any objectives they might set. (5 marks)

ⓔ 'Explain' means to show how the mission statement differs from objectives. The key is to relate the answer clearly to the case of Joe and Gina.

(d) Analyse the importance to Joe and Gina of setting clear objectives for their business. (9 marks)

ⓔ 'Analyse' means to develop a line of argument in this case related to clear (SMART) objectives for their business. Two key points to remember are that the answer must be set specifically in the context of Joe and Gina's business and that a question that stipulates 'analyse' does not require any judgement to be made.

(e) To what extent do you agree with Gina that survival is the most important objective over the first 3 years? Justify your view. (16 marks)

ⓔ 'To what extent' requires a judgement to be made. Balance is important, and for this question, you might look at two arguments why you might agree with Gina, two arguments why you might not, and finally come to a justified conclusion, perhaps saving a final piece of evidence to reinforce and really justify your view.

Student A

> **(a)** Profit is the reward for taking the risk of setting up in business. Time for Coffee is a new business just starting out and, although they might survive a few years making a loss, Joe and Gina will need profit in the long term to continue. This will also enable them to achieve their objective of establishing new outlets in neighbouring towns.

ⓔ **4/4 marks awarded.** This student has started by demonstrating an understanding of profit and shown why it is important to Joe and Gina. Time for Coffee is a new business that might be seeking to grow in the future.

(b) Year 2: 67,500 – 67,000 = £500 profit

Year 3: 80,000 – 72,000 = £8,000 profit

Increase in profit = £7,500

$$\frac{7,500}{500} \times 100 = 1,500\% \text{ increase in profit}$$

🄴 **6/6 marks awarded.** Although this student has not given a formula, the percentage increase in profit has been correctly calculated and full marks are awarded.

(c) Gina and Joe's mission statement represents their overall philosophy for the business. They want to be the best where people can have time to relax and time for themselves. This should, in time, give them a great reputation. Objectives, however, are targets to be achieved within a timeframe from which they can judge their success. So their projection of 10,000 customers in the first year would be a target from which at the end of the year they could judge how successful they had been.

🄴 **5/5 marks awarded.** This student has demonstrated a good understanding of both mission statements and objectives and clearly set them in the context of the case. A good answer.

(d) When setting objectives or targets for their business, Joe and Gina need to make sure these are SMART: specific, measurable, achievable, realistic and time-based. The objectives need to be clear because they have a number of important uses.

First, they should be motivating: if Joe and Gina have clear targets that are realistic, they will be motivated to achieving them, particularly as this is likely to mean their new business Time for Coffee is more likely to be successful.

Furthermore, targets can be used to evaluate the success of a business and judge how well it is doing. Joe and Gina have estimated customer numbers to be 10,000 in the first year and the average spend to be £5. Using this, they can see whether they have actually achieved their expected customer numbers and also whether their estimated spend was in fact £5. This then enables Joe and Gina to set up dated targets for the next year so that they are always SMART and motivational.

🄴 **8/9 marks awarded.** This is a good answer set in context and linking ideas from the case together, such as average spend and customer numbers. The second argument in particular is also well developed, although the application in this case is probably stronger than the analysis.

(e) There are arguments both for and against Gina's view. First, to some extent Gina, is correct. Time for Coffee is a new business that will take time to establish brand awareness and gain a reputation that will make customers choose their café over others. They might think they are conservative in estimating 10,000 customers in the first year, but this might turn out to be very optimistic and it does seem dependent on developments and growth in the tourist trade which may not happen as quickly as expected. Growth figures are predictions and just because the council has given the green light for developments it does not mean they will happen straight away.

On the other hand, bearing in mind there is little competition at the moment and if Joe and Gina can provide the atmosphere their mission statement suggests, they could very quickly establish a reputation for themselves even perhaps without the growth in visitor numbers. Also, if developments in attractions do take place, it is not unreasonable to expect visitor numbers to increase and footfall through the café to grow considerably.

Overall, however, I tend to agree with Gina: it is, after all, a brand-new business and there can be no guarantees. Although there are promises of greater visitor numbers, these are based on new developments which invariably take time to achieve. They would therefore be best to ensure their survival before thinking about anything else.

🄮 **16/16 marks awarded.** Again, a good answer, well planned and thought through with well-developed arguments set in the context of the case both for and against. Finally, there is a well-considered conclusion that is fully justified by the arguments made.

🄮 **Total score: 39/40 marks = a top grade A. Overall, this student has provided an excellent response that should easily achieve the top grade.**

Student B

(a) Profit is calculated as total revenue – total costs and is important for all businesses as without it they are likely to fail.

🄮 **2/4 marks awarded.** This student has an understanding of profit, but has not suggested *why* profit is important to Joe and Gina. In other words, there is no application to the case.

(b) Profit = revenue – total costs

Year 2: 67,500 – (40,000 + 27,000) = £500
Year 3: 80,000 – (40,000 + 32,000) = £8,000

Difference = £7,500

🄮 **4/6 marks awarded.** This is an incomplete answer. The profits for years 2 and 3 have been calculated and the difference found, but the percentage increase over the period has not been calculated. A good understanding of profit is demonstrated by both formula and correct calculations, and credit would be given for this.

(c) Joe and Gina's mission statement is 'Time for Coffee: time to enjoy, time to relax in the comfort and knowledge we are here to provide a first-class service.' This is an overall statement for what they are about. It differs from their objectives as their objectives are actual targets for what they want to achieve.

🅔 **2/5 marks awarded.** Again, this student provides an understanding of the terms in the question but has not related this to Joe and Gina.

(d) It is important for Joe and Gina to set clear objectives as first they need a clear target to work towards. Knowing they have a set target for customers is likely to motivate them to achieve that target and give them a sense of satisfaction and pride if they achieve it. It is important, however, that their targets are not too easily achieved and they must be set at the right level — not too difficult and not too easy.

Targets should in fact be SMART: specific, measurable, achievable, realistic and time-based. If they set a figure for sales, this will be specific. It can be measured by the value of sales achieved and they can set a time period for it. After that time period, they can then evaluate how they have done and decide what their future targets should be. Clear targets enable Joe and Gina to see how well they are doing, making it easier to judge the overall success of the business.

🅔 **4/9 marks awarded.** The first impression of this answer is that it lacks planning. It also lacks application to the case. In the first paragraph, there is some knowledge with limited development and where they start to talk about targets being achievable they have remembered targets should be SMART. The second paragraph is better, with a line of argument related to SMART targets and judging success. This is reasonable analysis.

(e) I agree with Gina that survival is the most important objective in the early years. Very few new businesses are successful in the first few years and many make losses due to the fact the costs of setting up have been high. This is because new businesses take time to establish a reputation, brand loyalty and the resultant repeat custom. Time for Coffee would find it difficult to start with as no one would know they existed and they would have to do lots of advertising which could be costly, making it even more difficult to be successful.

It is possible that Joe could be right — they might do much better than expected — but they would have to gain a lot of customers to do so and I don't see this happening for a new business who would be competing with already existing cafés anyway.

Overall, I would agree with Gina in that survival should be their top priority over the first few years.

(e) **6/16 marks awarded.** This student clearly has a problem with application as, once again, the arguments made are not set in the context of the case. Just mentioning the name of the business or a piece of detail from the case does not in itself make for application. For application to be present, some detail from the case must be used effectively in an argument. Although this student recognises the need to look at both sides of the argument, only the supporting case is developed to a reasonable level. The judgement made is also limited and lacking in real detail.

(e) **Total score: 18/40 marks = a low pass grade. Overall, this student has produced a weak response that might achieve a grade E but no more.**

Question 2 Barnard's Boats Ltd

Barnard's Boats Ltd is a family-run business started by James and now run by his two sons, Morgan and Ivan. It has been operating successfully for over 25 years. In fact, in many ways, it has been a victim of its own success as it has grown significantly from its early days of producing small boats in one yard on the River Solent. It now has three separate yards which, although sufficient, causes considerable logistical difficulties in terms of resources and extra costs. Most importantly, however, none were capable of building the bigger yachts for which there was an increasing demand and which commanded potentially higher profit margins.

The company has reached a crossroads: should it try to accommodate the changing market or should it stay as it is. This decision is all the more imperative now as an opportunity had arisen to purchase a new prime site that would enable it to satisfy all its production needs at one site for the foreseeable future. However, this would not be a cheap option and a rough estimate indicates that the site and fitting out for production would cost at least £15m. Although the company might raise £5m from its existing sites, this money would not be available until it is up and running at a new site.

Morgan and Ivan are convinced that the opportunity to purchase a new yard should be grasped and feel that a move to the stock market as a public limited company may be the answer. The business has been financially sound for a number of years. Despite the recession, they have succeeded in making a small profit in all but one year. Orders are now once again picking up and there have been numerous enquiries regarding the larger yachts they are unable to build. Going public would provide them with the capital they require and enable the business to compete in a much wider market. A brief chat with their accountant indicates that they might be able to raise close to £10m from a share issue of 49% of the business, with the remainder of the money coming from retained profit and a small bank loan.

James, their father, is more sceptical — although he is very much in the background, the company is still his pride and joy. It would not be a family business any more and it would be answerable to shareholders. Clearly, he is going to take some convincing that a floatation is the right move for the business.

(a) Barnard's Boats is already an incorporated business. Explain what this means for the owners. (4 marks)

ⓔ A possible approach for students answering this question is to outline how being an incorporated business is different from being uncorporated for the owners.

(b) Explain the likely impact of a recession on Barnard's Boats. (6 marks)

ⓔ The key to full marks for this question is to make sure that any explanation is clearly related to Barnard's Boats.

(c) Analyse the benefits to Barnard's Boats of becoming a public limited company. (9 marks)

ⓔ 'Analyse' means to provide a developed argument of the benefits of plc status to Barnard's Boats.

(d) To what extent do you believe an investment in Barnard's Boats would be a good one for shareholders? Justify your view. (15 marks)

ⓔ 'To what extent' means to provide a judgement and requires some weighing up of the arguments both for and against this being a good investment before arriving at a justified conclusion.

(e) James is clearly not convinced that becoming a plc is the answer. To what extent do you think he is correct in his opinion? Justify your view. (16 marks)

ⓔ As with the previous question, a judgement needs to be made. Arguments on both sides need to be considered before arriving at a justified conclusion.

Student A

(a) Incorporation means a business has been incorporated under the Companies Act and is recognised legally as being separate from the owners of the business. For Barnard's Boats this means they have limited liability and their own personal possessions cannot be taken to pay the debts of the business.

ⓔ **4/4 marks awarded.** A good answer demonstrating a sound understanding of incorporation as well as illustrating what it means for the owners of Barnard's Boats.

(b) A recession is a period of two consecutive quarters of negative growth in the economy. This means that demand is likely to fall, particularly for luxury items such as boats, as consumers have less disposable income. That said, Barnard's Boats appears to be less affected than some businesses and this might be because its target market is likely to be the very wealthy who are perhaps less affected and more likely to continue spending. As a result, the company continued to make a profit through the recession.

ⓔ 6/6 marks awarded. Not only has this student got a full grasp of what a recession is, this has also been applied fully in the context of Barnard's Boats. This is reinforced by the idea that wealthier people are less affected by a recession, which explains why the business continued to make a profit during the recent recession. A very good answer.

(c) There are a number of benefits to Barnard's Boats of becoming a plc. The most important benefit to the owners perhaps is the access to much greater amounts of capital. If Morgan and Ivan are to purchase the new site, this will cost £15m. To borrow this amount attracts high interest payments, which adds to the costs and threatens the business's profitability and financial security. By raising £10m through shares, this alleviates the problem of high interest payments and still leaves them in control of the business as they will keep 51% of the shares. As a public limited company Barnard's Boats may also be viewed by suppliers and creditors as more reliable and stable, which may enable the business to gain better credit terms, further helping its financial position.

ⓔ 9/9 marks awarded. This is a good answer. It keeps very much to the question, making well-developed arguments for becoming a plc, and these arguments are set fully in the context of Barnard's Boats.

(d) Shareholders invest for two main reasons: income and capital growth. By income, they want a share of any profit each year as a dividend, and by capital growth they hope that the overall value of their shares will go up (share price × number of shares). So what chance have Barnard's Boats got of achieving this? First, the company is a profitable business: even during the recession, it continued to make a profit and, with demand now increasing, profits should begin to rise again. This should give encouragement to shareholders for both potential dividends and, as business picks up, capital growth due to a rising share price. This is just based on their current three-site business: if they were to move to one site, profit could be much higher because of the expected cost reductions and, if as expected they could gain orders for bigger boats with higher profit margins, there is every reason to expect growing profit, dividends and capital growth.

Every investment, however, carries a risk and there can be no guarantees in business. Will the expected cost reductions materialise and will Barnard's Boats gain any orders for bigger boats? As an investor, it would be good to see assurances on these things. Also, although we are told that the business has been profitable, we are not given any indication of how profitable and therefore the likely dividend that could be expected. As an investor, it would be necessary to see financial projections for the future before committing money to an investment such as this.

Overall, an investment in this business has every chance of being a good one. The accountant feels it is a good move, the economy is coming out of recession and everything seems in place for Barnard's Boats to continue to improve on its profitable business.

ℯ **15/15 marks awarded.** This answer provides a good example of a well-considered, planned answer. The first paragraph in particular is well developed and fully in the context of the case. The second paragraph is also good and the final conclusion and judgement seem to be fully justified by the answer.

> **(e)** I feel that James has good reason to be sceptical of the move to plc status, but I believe him to be wrong in this view. As it says in the case study, the business is his pride and joy: he set it up and probably feels it will no longer be a family business once it becomes a plc. In some ways he may be correct in this as the business will to some extent become answerable to the needs of shareholders and will need to impress the City if the share price is to be maintained and grow.
>
> Barnard's Boats, however, has a choice to make: does it wish to stay as it is and just trundle along making some profit but with little opportunity to grow and expand the business, or does it want to become a much bigger and hopefully more profitable business altogether? If it is the latter, this is a once-in-a-lifetime opportunity — a chance to get the bigger yard they need. If they don't take this opportunity now, it might never come up again. It comes at a cost, but by selling shares the owners are actually reducing the financial pressures compared to a loan.
>
> Furthermore, although James is worried about the family losing control of the business, this will not happen as they are selling off only 49% of the business. This means the family will hold 51% of the shares and have a controlling interest over all decisions made. Yes, there might be some pressure from the City and shareholders, but there is no reason to see this as a threat as they are a profitable business with the likelihood of becoming even more profitable in the future, which would curry favour with City analysts.
>
> Overall, although it is easy to understand the father's concerns, I believe he need not be particularly worried. If he wishes to see the company grow and prosper in the future, becoming a public limited company and buying the new site seems to be the answer. There could be even more reason for him to be proud of the business he started in the years to come.

ℯ **16/16 marks awarded.** This student continues to give the impression of carefully planning his answers. Both sides of the argument are once again considered and developed in context and the final conclusion is fully justified.

ℯ **Total score: 50/50 marks = a top grade A. It is difficult to fault this student, who gives an excellent answer that would have no problem achieving a top grade.**

Student B

(a) Incorporation means they are a limited company and have limited liability.

ⓔ 2/4 marks awarded. This student shows just some understanding of incorporation here, with no attempt to demonstrate what it means to the owners of Barnard's Boats.

(b) A recession is a period of falling demand, unemployment tends to rise and people generally have less disposable income. As a result, demand for luxury items tends to be hit the hardest as consumers tend to focus on necessities. So Barnard's Boats is likely to see a fall in demand and will probably even make a loss.

ⓔ 3/6 marks awarded. This student understands what is meant by recession but has made a limited attempt to apply it to the case.

(c) Becoming a plc has a number of benefits and drawbacks. The biggest benefit to Barnard's Boats is the access to greater amounts of capital. If it is to buy the new site, it needs £15m which is a lot of money that would be difficult to get from loan. On top of which the loan would require large amounts of interest to be paid, which could cause serious financial and cash-flow problems for the business.

Becoming a plc, however, does have its problems as Barnard's Boats would become answerable to shareholders, many of whom are only interested in short-term profit. It is also possible that the family may no longer have control of the business, especially if they sell off more shares in the future.

Overall, I believe becoming a plc is the best thing for Barnard's Boats to do as it will give the owners the chance to buy the new yard they so obviously need.

ⓔ 5/9 marks awarded. A common mistake by students in this type of question, which requires analysis of the *benefits*, is to look at both benefits and drawbacks. No reward is given for development of the drawbacks. The first paragraph, however, demonstrates a reasonable attempt at developing a relevant argument in context.

(d) I think investment in Barnard's Boats would be a good one for shareholders. It is a profitable business and even during the recession it did not make a loss and so there is every reason to believe it will continue to make profit in the future. Also, orders should go up now the recession is over, which should mean increased profit. If it operates on one site, this should reduce its costs and make building boats a whole lot easier, which again should help reduce costs and therefore achieve higher profit. Since shareholders look for high returns from their investments, Barnard's Boats should be able to achieve this.

Nothing is guaranteed, however, and investors should research any potential investment carefully before putting money in. They should also be aware that consumer tastes might change: bigger boats may go out of fashion or the economy could be hit by recession again, both of which could significantly reduce demand for boats and reduce business profits. As a result, an investment in this business could be very risky.

Overall, I believe an investment in this business would be a good one. Any investment carries a risk and from what I said in my first paragraph this looks more likely to be a success.

(e) **7/15 marks awarded.** The first paragraph is an interesting one as there are a number of ideas put forward but they are written almost as separate points rather than a developed argument. The second paragraph puts forward a counter-argument, but the application to the case is limited. The arguments overall could have been better developed, trying to link aspects from the case. The final judgement, although having some support, could also have been developed further.

(e) In some ways, although the father plays little part in the business, he probably still feels it is his and that his sons are selling it off. As a result, it will no longer be a family business. It will be controlled by shareholders rather than the family and they will only be interested in making a profit. There is probably some truth in this, but as they are only selling 49% of the business they should still have overall control and their say should be final in any decisions.

Whether they become a plc or not probably depends on whether they wish to go ahead with the purchase of the new site, which is probably dependent on their objectives for the future. If their objective is to grow rather than just survive, then they need to purchase the new site and the best way to do this is to become a plc.

Overall, I do not think the father should be at all worried about Barnard's Boats becoming a plc because if he wants to see his business move to the next stage in its life it would appear to be the logical thing to do.

(e) **10/16 marks awarded.** This student makes an attempt to develop his arguments and there is some context to the answer, but only at a reasonable level. There is also some support for the judgement made, but again this is only reasonable.

(e) **Total score: 27/50 marks = a low pass grade. Part (e) provides a reasonable response, but the overall quality of this answer is rather weak. Having said that, Student B has probably said enough to achieve a D grade.**

Question 3 Trumps Travel Ltd

Trumps Travel has reached the landmark of 50 years of operating in the travel business, offering inexpensive holidays to discerning customers. This, however, is not a happy anniversary: sales over the last 5 years have been showing a downward trend and what had been a very profitable business is now making a loss. On the one hand, the recent recession has caused demand to fall and, on the other hand, there has been a significant move away from high street shops to online booking, both of which the business had been ill prepared for.

Until now, Trumps Travel has always appointed a new CEO from within, taking the view that someone who is already with the organisation would have their finger on the pulse and a better understanding of the business. This is about to change with the appointment of Andy Riddick, a no-nonsense chief executive who has a particular interest and experience in the online sales industry and comes with a reputation of sorting out ailing companies. He is not one for lengthy discussions and, although he might let others have their say, once he has made up his mind that is usually it. His appointment is not a popular one among most of the board.

Andy was first contacted 6 months ago by one of the current board of directors and had already done some homework on the business. Some harsh decisions would need to be made: some of the less well-performing shops in smaller towns and cities would need to be closed, with inevitable job losses. Although Andy believes that the external environment and, in particular, the economy are crucial factors in the performance of Trumps Travel, he also believes that a travel business can prosper even in difficult economic times.

A key aspect for Andy is the online business and he plans an increased spending on this with a complete revamp of the website. Up to now, the website has been developed in-house and, although functional, it is far from being the best in the market. His aim is to make the website the best and the most user-friendly in the sector as he sees the online route as the way forward. His idea is to use a consultancy firm to develop a new website, but this means even more redundancies. He will need to convince the directors that this is the best way forward and, to this end, he has produced a decision tree. He has been able to establish the cost of each option, in-house or outside consultancy firm, and estimate the probabilities of a good, medium and poor outcome for each option. Using the consultancy firm appears to offer the best results. Would the other directors be convinced by this?

(a) Explain the role of Andy Riddick as the leader of Trumps Travel. (4 marks)

ⓔ This question requires the student to identify the role of a leader and set it in the context of Trumps Travel. A common mistake is to develop arguments in detail with analysis. This is not necessary for a question that asks students to explain.

(b) Using the evidence from the case study, explain where you would place Andy on the Tannenbaum Schmidt continuum and the Blake Mouton grid. (6 marks)

ⓔ This question tests the students' understanding of these two models. All that is required is for candidates to place Andy in each of models using evidence from the case study to explain their choice of positioning.

(c) Analyse the potential benefits to Trumps Travel of Andy's style of leadership. (9 marks)

ⓔ It is important that students only develop the benefits of this leadership style and not the drawbacks.

(d) To what extent do you believe Andy's use of a decision tree to be effective in deciding who should develop the new website? Using evidence from the case study justify your view. (15 marks)

ⓔ 'To what extent' means to make a judgement. The reasons for and against the effectiveness of decision trees in this case can be put forward and an overall justified conclusion made.

(e) Andy believes that the external environment is the key influence on his decision-making. To what extent to you agree? Justify your view. (16 marks)

ⓔ This is a broad question and the key to answering it is to be selective. Which of the external environment factors would have most influence on Trumps Travel? Perhaps look at two areas as well as another non-external factor before coming to a justified conclusion.

Student A

(a) The role of a leader is to analyse situations, set objectives, make decisions and review the situation. It is important for Trumps Travel that Andy can do this as the business is struggling and he needs to analyse why, and make decisions in order to revive its position. This is what he has been appointed for.

ⓔ **4/4 marks awarded.** This is a good answer. The role of a leader is clearly identified and set in the context of Trumps Travel.

(b) The Tannenbaum Schmidt continuum and the Blake Mouton grid are both models of leadership. On the Tannenbaum Schmidt continuum, Andy is very much on the left-hand side, telling people what to do. Although he lets others have their say, he is the one who decides — once he has made up his mind that is it. On the Blake Mouton grid he probably falls into task management as he is more concerned with the end result rather than the people he is working with. He does let them have a say, but his decision is final.

ⓔ **6/6 marks awarded.** A good answer — there is no doubt that this student understands these two models of leadership and evidence from the case is used to place Andy's style within each.

(c) Andy's style of leadership appears to be autocratic, which can be useful in some situations. Decision-making is likely to be quick as there are no committees and lengthy discussions. The situation is assessed by the leader and the decision made. Trumps Travel is obviously undergoing difficult times and it needs to make decisions quickly otherwise the situation will only get worse and it will fall further behind the competition. Therefore, this style could be good for the business.

In addition, in the past Trumps Travel has always appointed a CEO from within the organisation, which means Andy as an 'outsider' who is highly likely to meet with considerable opposition and a more democratic style might lead to lengthy discussion and indecision. The best way for Andy to overcome this may well be a more autocratic style, particularly at first. If he can make the right decisions, prove himself and lead the recovery of Trumps Travel, he could well gain the respect of others. Although there are significant disadvantages of this style of leadership, given the circumstances Trumps Travel finds itself in this may well be the best style to overcome its problems.

e **9/9 marks awarded.** This is a well-considered answer. Andy's style of leadership is identified and the benefits are put forward in a well-reasoned argument that is fully in the context of Trumps Travel, i.e. the opposition from board members and its struggling position.

(d) Decision trees are a form of scientific management that can help to reduce the risk in decision-making. They use estimated returns and probabilities to calculate the financial outcome of a decision. Having quantitative data to help support an argument can give weight to the argument being made and increase the chances of success of a decision. Andy has undertaken such analysis for the development of the website, which seems to suggest using outside consultants is the best way forward.

However, Andy wants to use outside consultants so his view of estimates and probabilities may well be biased toward this decision. He produces favourable figures because this is what he wants and he hopes it will sway the other directors to his view. Another problem revolves around on what he bases his estimates and probabilities as Trumps Travel has never done anything like this before so there is no past data. Perhaps he is using figures from other firms he has been involved with — the case study says he has experience in the online sales industry — but although useful these may not be related to the travel industry.

Overall, decision trees certainly have their uses and can be effective in helping to reduce risk, but in this case I believe their effectiveness is limited. This is due to the fact I believe Andy is trying to force his own view on the rest of the board and so he facilitates a favourable outcome and there is no past evidence to base any of the figures on. He is probably well aware of the board's opposition to him and thinks using scientific decision-making will give added weight to what he wants to do.

e **13/15 marks awarded.** This answer has all the hallmarks of a well-planned and balanced answer. The first paragraph not only demonstrates a clear understanding of decision trees, it also develops the reasons for Andy using such analysis. The second paragraph addresses the drawbacks of such analysis. The final paragraph draws the answer together, coming to and justifying the conclusion that in this case a decision tree may be of limited use. The application in this answer is stronger than the analysis so it might not achieve full marks, but it is nevertheless a strong answer.

(e) The external environment includes those areas outside the control of the business such as the economy and competition, and changing tastes and fashion. These are important areas that have big influence on the performance of a business. Andy cannot control what happens in the economy, the changing tastes and fashions or what competitors are doing. All he can do is try to anticipate and move with the times. It was the recession and the move by consumers to online booking that caused the decline in performance of Trumps Travel and any future changes in the economy could have a big impact on the business, both negative and positive.

It is not only external factors that can affect business performance; other factors can also. The availability of finance for any changes to be made will most certainly affect success. If not enough money is available for developing the new website, the quality of the final result may not be as good. This is of particular importance to Trumps Travel as it wants its website to be the best in the business. Also, success can be influenced by the quality of personnel and it may be essential that a consultancy firm is employed to produce the website as it is more likely to have the necessary skills to make the website the best in the business.

Overall, to some extent Andy is correct in stating that external influences are key to success, but a business should nonetheless anticipate changes and be prepared to move with changing circumstances. Sometimes it may not be the changing external environment that leads to problems but a business culture that is reluctant to change. Culture, finance and the skills of personnel are all internal factors that may also be key influences on decision-making. In any given situation, it could be either external, internal or a combination of both that affect the success of a decision.

🅔 **13/16 marks awarded.** A nicely balanced answer that addresses both the influence of external and internal factors. The arguments are well developed, set in the context of the business and the conclusion is well considered. This answer may not quite achieve full marks, but it is certainly an excellent response.

🅔 **Total score: 45/50 marks = a top grade A. An overall excellent response that would have little problem in achieving a top grade.**

Student B

(a) The role of a leader is to lead the business out of trouble by looking at its problems, making decisions and reviewing what happens. This is very important for Trumps Travel as it is a struggling business.

🅔 **3/4 marks awarded.** The role of a leader is identified and a limited attempt made to apply this to Trumps Travel. The awarded 3 marks may be a little generous.

(b) The Tannenbaum Schmidt continuum looks at leadership in a range from autocratic decision-making at one end to full freedom at the other end, whereas the Blake Mouton grid places a leader within a grid with concern for others on the *y*-axis and concern for task/production on the *x*-axis. Andy appears to be an autocratic leader.

ⓔ 2/6 marks awarded. The models are well understood and, although Andy has been identified as an autocratic leader, his position within the two theories has not been made clear.

(c) Trumps Travel is going through a difficult period and action is needed urgently to put things right. Andy's style of leadership is likely to upset members of the board who are not happy with his appointment. His style therefore can be very demotivating. However, sometimes difficult decisions do need to be made. Many people will not be happy to be made redundant and it will take a particular type of leader to push such decisions through. Andy's style, which appears to be very autocratic, may well be the best style in this situation to get the results required.

ⓔ 4/9 marks awarded. This answer adopts an unusual approach. The first part appears to focus on the problems of Andy's style and only in the final sentence, where it is suggested that this style of leadership may be the best in difficult circumstances such as this, is the answer brought together.

(d) Decision trees are branch-like diagrams that can be used in decision-making. Andy has undertaken this in order to help in the decision of whether the new website should be designed in-house or whether an outside consultant should be used. He has worked out the costs and estimated the probabilities of good, medium and poor returns. This shows that outside consultants would be the best decision. The benefit of doing this is that it reduces risk and makes the chance of success much more likely.

On the other hand, decision trees do have their drawbacks. Nothing can completely eliminate risk, circumstances can change and the expected returns may never happen. The probabilities used are often only estimates and are not based on real figures, so their chances of actually matching actual outcomes are slim.

Overall, using decision trees can be useful and they should help Andy in this case as it reduces the risk of getting it wrong. This is something Trumps Travel cannot afford to do as it could end up in an even worse position than before.

ⓔ 7/15 marks awarded. This answer has a good structure in that it looks at the benefits and drawbacks of decision trees and then draws a conclusion. However, the arguments could be developed in more detail and set in the context of Trumps Travel. The lack of context (application) also prevents any meaningful judgement being made on the question asked.

(e) The external environment can be a big influence on decision-making. Competitors' actions can affect the performance of a business, perhaps by the introduction of a new product or a new marketing campaign that captures market share from Trumps Travel. The economy can seriously affect the performance of a travel business as something like a recession can reduce consumer disposable income and cause a lack of demand for holidays or consumers to change their preferences to holidays at home rather than holidays abroad.

As well as this, consumer tastes and fashion might change, perhaps from Mediterranean holidays to holidays further afield. It may be that government action such as increased fuel duties or airport duty could affect the cost of holidays and therefore demand. All these things can be a key influence on decision-making.

Environmental issues can also be a key influence. Consumers are much more socially aware today. As a result of opinions about global warming, they might decide to cut back on long-haul holiday flights or have a holiday at home instead of flying off somewhere.

There are many external influences on a business such as Trumps Travel and Andy is probably right that one way or another these will be key in any decision-making.

e **7/16 marks awarded.** This answer focuses solely on the external factors. The student has tried to mention as many as possible and as a result none is developed in detail. The judgement made is also weak and lacking in justification.

e **Total score: 23/50 marks = a low pass grade. This student has struggled to come to terms with this particular exercise and the best that could be hoped for in terms of grade is an E.**

Question 4 Skifest Scotland

The future of Skifest Scotland, an organisation that operates a ski centre in the Grampians in Scotland, has come under increasing threat over recent years. Although last winter was a little better in terms of snow, there was only a small increase in visitor numbers and the overall trend was still down. Extrapolation of the trend line indicated that Skifest Scotland would be unable to continue in business within 5 years and it did not need a marketing expert to reveal the positive correlation of a lack of snow to visitor numbers. Clearly if it were to remain in business, snow sports would not be the complete answer.

Managing director Ana Manne feels that the lack of guarantees about snow and the wider and easier availability of skiing in Europe and further afield is limiting the business's target market to a small group local enthusiasts. What is needed is something that appeals to a wider target audience and offers a year-round attraction rather than Skifest Scotland's current, very seasonal, business. The ideas she has come up with are all aimed at making use of the organisation's natural resource — the mountains and lochs — and include mountain biking, climbing, kayaking, hiking and guided walks through the mountains.

The activity that has perhaps most appeal is mountain biking. A recent study for the BBC indicates that the market is growing by 30% a year and it is estimated to be worth over £119m to the Scottish economy. Compared to skiing, which lacks growth and is worth at best £25m a year, it is easy to see why Ana is so excited by this research data. Further to this she has researched the information in Table 2 for mountain bike events.

Her current thinking is to set up an activity-based visitor attraction focusing initially on mountain biking, but if it is successful then to branch into other activities catering for a wider target audience. The terrain is ideally suited for trails and the development of tracks for competitions. At the moment, this is all based on limited secondary research and the next step is to undertake her own primary research. Even so, Ana already feels she is on to a winner.

Year	Volume	Value
2008	32,188	£739,918
2010	40,659	£1,106,180
2012	53,600	£1,510,320

Table 2 Competitive mountain bike events

(a) Calculate the growth in value of competitive mountain bike events between 2008 and 2012. (5 marks)

e A common mistake students make with this type of question is that they do not use the correct figures for the calculation. It is the figures for 'value' between 2008 and 2012 that should be used here.

(b) Explain the terms 'extrapolation' and 'correlation' in relation to Skifest Scotland. (5 marks)

e This question requires students to show they understand the terms as they might be used in the context of Skifest Scotland.

(c) Analyse the disadvantages to Skifest Scotland of having such a limited target market. (9 marks)

e The answer here should focus on the disadvantages only and must be developed in the context of Skifest Scotland and its target market of snow-sport enthusiasts.

(d) At the moment, Ana has only undertaken secondary research. Evaluate the importance of conducting additional primary market research. (15 marks)

e The focus of this question should be the usefulness of primary research as opposed to secondary research and in particular why it is essential for Skifest Scotland. It is an evaluation question so a judgement should be made.

(e) To what extent do you agree with Ana that a move to mountain biking would be a winning move? Justify your answer. (16 marks)

e This is an evaluation question and in this case consideration should be given to both sides of the argument with a clear judgement as to whether Ana is correct in her view or not.

> **Student A**
>
> **(a)** Growth of the market = $\dfrac{739{,}918 - 1{,}510{,}320}{739{,}918} \times 100$
>
> $= 104.12\%$

ⓔ 5/5 marks awarded. This is the correct answer, scoring full marks.

> **(b)** Extrapolation and correlation are useful tools in business. In terms of Skifest Scotland, it is quite easy to understand them as the trend in visitors has been declining because of a lack of snow. If that rate of decline is extended (extrapolated) into the future, a prediction can be made for future number of visitors. This represents a positive correlation between the amount of snow and visitor numbers.

ⓔ 5/5 marks awarded. This is a good answer demonstrating a clear understanding of the terms and set fully in the context of Skifest Scotland.

> **(c)** A businesses target market is the group of customers it aims it product or service at. Sometimes this might be the whole market or, as in this case, a particular segment or niche in the market, that of snow-sports enthusiasts. Skifest Scotland has a limited target market and, although this can sometimes be beneficial, in this case it has become a real disadvantage. This is not just because the market itself is quite small, it is also because the key ingredient it relies upon — snow — has been in very short supply. By limiting itself to such a small group, the company is limiting its ability to generate revenue and therefore profit and could find itself out of business within 5 years. On top of this the company is faced with increasingly cheaper holidays to Europe and beyond, where snow can be guaranteed, so its target market is getting even smaller.

ⓔ 8/9 marks awarded. This is a very good answer. There is a clear understanding of the target market and a disadvantage is discussed fully in the context of Skifest Scotland. The application is perhaps stronger then the analysis, preventing full marks but still gaining a creditable 8 marks.

> **(d)** Primary market research is first-hand research that can be specifically tailored to the needs of a business. This is why it is so important to a business. It is all very well looking at figures for the growth in mountain biking, but would people be prepared to travel to Scotland for it and what sort of facilities and tracks would they like? If Ana could collect information on this type of thing, it would give the business the best possible chance of establishing the sort of facility consumers would come to in large numbers. It is also important to collect information from the local area. Changing from snow sports to a year-round facility that might damage the

environment could encounter real opposition. It would be really useful to know just how much opposition Skifest Scotland would encounter, enabling it to put together plans in such a way to keep people happy. Ana might do this by establishing small focus groups to gauge feelings about the project.

Clearly, primary market research is important to a business: Ana would struggle to get her ideas up and running without it. To go ahead, Skifest Scotland would need finance and investors would need solid facts on the likely visitor numbers, jobs created, impact on environment etc. Just because the growth in the market suggests success, this would not be enough on its own to convince investors and as a result primary market research is essential.

🄯 **15/15 marks awarded.** An excellent answer, set fully in the context of Skifest Scotland. A number of arguments are developed and the final conclusion is well evaluated with the link to the need to raise finance.

(e) Skifest Scotland is a business that, if it continues to focus only on snow sports, is likely to be out of business within the next 5 years. It is reliant on snow for success and this has been in short supply. In addition, it is so much easier to travel to Europe and get guaranteed good snow, so why would anyone come to Scotland to ski? As it stands, it is a seasonal business with a limited target market that is shrinking. By broadening its activities to mountain biking and perhaps other activities, it would no longer be a seasonal business and instead it would have the ability to generate revenue throughout the year. On top of this, its target market would be wider and it is growing by 30% a year. The mountain terrain would also be ideal for mountain biking and in particular competitions. In many ways, this does look like a winning formula.

Ana would not have first-mover advantage, however, and she would have to persuade the planners to get the go-ahead, all of which could mean this may not be viable.

Overall, because of the large market growth and the move to a year-round business, providing she can be up and running quickly I believe this to be a winning formula for Skifest Scotland. Without it, the company is likely to be out of business anyway.

🄯 **13/16 marks awarded.** This student was perhaps running out of time toward the end of this answer as the counter-argument is quite brief — one sentence. However, the argument in support of mountain biking in the first paragraph is well developed and fully in context, and worthy of a good mark. Without the balance of a stronger counter-argument, it is difficult to fully justify the claim so some marks are lost in terms of evaluation. Overall, though, still a good mark.

🄯 **Total score: 46/50 marks = a top grade A. This student has provided a consistently excellent response that would have little problem achieving a top grade.**

(a) $\dfrac{32{,}188 - 53{,}600}{32{,}188} = 0.665$

ⓔ 0/5 marks awarded. This student has made the mistake of using the volume figures rather than the value figures. She has also not worked it out as a percentage — had she done, so it might have been possible to award 1 mark for a correct formula.

(b) Extrapolation means to extend a trend line on a chart in order to forecast future visitor numbers. Correlation means to compare one thing to another to see if they are positively or negatively related (correlated). For example, there might be a positive correlation between the level of advertising and visitor numbers.

ⓔ 3/5 marks awarded. This student has a good understanding of these terms but has not set them in the context of Skifest Scotland other than a passing reference to visitor numbers.

(c) Businesses sell their product to a group of customers and this is known as their target market. By knowing your target market it means any advertising can be directed specifically at that group which therefore enables the business to save costs. In Skifest Scotland's case, its target market is quite small and probably younger people who enjoy skiing and snowboarding.

This does have its disadvantages because it means its market is limited to only a small group of people, which means any decline in demand has a big impact on the business's profitability. This is what Skifest Scotland is finding at the moment: numbers have dropped and if that continues it will go out of business.

ⓔ 4/9 marks awarded. The first paragraph confirms this student's understanding of 'target market' but does little else, and the mention of an advantage is irrelevant. The second paragraph is better as it addresses a disadvantage, but it is quite weak.

(d) Secondary market research is desk research using information that has already been collected by someone else, whereas primary market research is field research collected directly for the purposes of the business. Secondary research is quite cheap to collect whereas primary can be very costly.

However, primary research does have a number of advantages in that it is specific to the needs of the business and can be effective in reducing the risk of decision-making. Primary market research could be undertaking questionnaires set specifically to the potential target market or for those people affected by the new development. Ana could also undertake focus groups to gain opinions from particular groups of people about how they might react to Skifest Scotland's ideas for development. This could be very important as there could be a big impact on the environment.

In evaluation, primary market research is essential if Ana is to go ahead with this development. First-hand information is essential in order to convince all those involved with such a move.

ⓔ 6/15 marks awarded. Overall, this is a weak response. The first paragraph introduces the terms and demonstrates understanding. The second outlines two particular methods of primary research and their advantages, but with only a very limited attempt at application. Why might there be a big environmental impact? The final sentence is an attempt at judgement but there is no justification.

(e) I believe Ana is right that mountain biking is a winning formula. At the moment, skiing is not looking good: numbers are falling and Skifest Scotland will soon be out of business. Mountain biking is popular, as shown by the rising numbers: 30% a year and the value of the market has shown over 100% growth in 4 years. To be a part of this market can only be good for business.

There is a chance that Ana could be wrong, however, as the mountains in Scotland can be quite remote and who is to say people will travel to the location? So although the market might be growing, there might be facilities within easier access to potential customers. She would have to establish a first-rate facility if she was going to get people to come: something with its own USP, perhaps a highly rated competitive track.

Overall, I believe this could be a winning formula for the business. As long as they can establish a first-rate facility, people will be prepared to travel.

ⓔ 9/16 marks awarded. This answer tries to look at both sides of the argument. The first paragraph gives reasons for agreeing with Ana: ideas are taken from the case study but the argument and analysis are quite weak as they are a series of points rather than developed into an argument. The second paragraph is a little better, suggesting it might be difficult to attract people to Scotland, and this does provide some justification for the conclusion in the final sentence.

ⓔ Total score: 22/50 marks = a low pass grade. A weak response that would struggle to achieve a pass grade. The best that could be hoped for would be a grade E.

Question 5 JetFast plc

JetFast is a well-known budget airline that has seen a small decline in profit for the first time in 5 years and its position as the leading budget airline taken by a rival company. Managing director Hal Bertrand is concerned that this might be the beginning of a worrying trend of decline and not just a one-off event.

When JetFast first started, the company benefitted from first-mover advantage in the budget airline market and a key element of its marketing mix was price. It considered consumers to be highly price sensitive and that they would react positively to lower prices. JetFast's no-frills service — often flying between lesser-known airports where landing fees were cheaper — enabled it to offer rock-bottom fares. Staff were also treated poorly, employed on zero-hours contracts and having to pay for their own uniforms. At first, this approach saw large numbers of consumers deciding to fly with JetFast, but things were now changing.

The market is now far more competitive, with a number of carriers offering similar prices and in some cases travelling to more convenient airports. On top of this, JetFast has gained a reputation of focusing purely on cost minimisation, charging extra for everything from baggage to using the toilet onboard.

One of its leading rivals seems to be profiting from offering a slightly more discerning service, still budget but with a good deal more convenience. This airline has undertaken some detailed primary market research, particularly in small focus groups where it collected the opinions of consumers in terms of what they wanted from a budget airline. Clearly, this company is taking a much broader view of the marketing mix and developing a marketing strategy that fully integrates all elements of the mix.

If JetFast is to regain its position as the leading budget airline, Hal believes a complete rethink on what the airline has to offer is required, not just in terms of marketing but also other functional areas such as operations and human resources.

(a) Explain the benefits JetFast might gain from using qualitative market research. (5 marks)

ⓔ 'Explain' means to show how qualitative market research will benefit JetFast. No analysis is required and the answer should be completely in the context of JetFast.

(b) A knowledge of price elasticity of demand can be a useful tool for a business. Explain how the management of JetFast might have used this knowledge in establishing the airline. (5 marks)

ⓔ This is also an 'explain' question that requires students to show how the management of JetFast might use a knowledge of elasticity. The answer must be focused on JetFast.

(c) Analyse the benefits to Hal of a knowledge of product life cycle in terms of developing a new marketing strategy. (9 marks)

ⓔ A common mistake in this type of question is that students develop lots of benefits. It is much better to develop one or two in detail than to try to cover lots of points briefly. Any benefit covered should be in the context of JetFast.

(d) To what extent do you believe price to be the most important element of a budget airline's marketing mix? Justify your view.　　　　　　　　(15 marks)

ⓔ Exam questions often ask students to consider whether one element of the marketing mix is more important than others. Common mistakes in such questions are that students focus only on that element, discussing it in general terms rather than in the context of the business — in this case, JetFast.

(e) Hal believes that if JetFast is to regain its position as the leading budget airline, a complete rethink is necessary, not just in terms of marketing but also the other functional areas of the business. To what extent do you agree with him? Justify your view.　　　　　　　　(16 marks)

ⓔ This question requires students to think about the marketing mix in the context of the other functional areas. In other words, it is about the integrated nature of business decision-making. The addition of the Ps of people and process provide an opportunity to develop an answer here, even if the other areas of the specification have yet to be covered.

Student A

(a) Qualitative research is all about collecting people's opinions and feelings about something, and is a form of primary market research. This can give JetFast an idea of what customers actually think about the airline and what they are looking for. One of its competitors has benefitted by responding to customer wants expressed in a focus group. Maybe JetFast should do the same as this could help it get away from the image of cost minimisation and lack of customer care.

ⓔ **5/5 marks awarded.** This answer demonstrates a clear understanding of qualitative market research and is set fully in the context of JetFast.

(b) Price elasticity of demand measures the responsiveness of demand to changes in price. If in calculating it an answer greater than 1 is achieved, the product or service is termed elastic in that a change in price will see a greater change in demand. So if prices are lowered, the effect on demand will lead to greater revenue and profit. It was perhaps a knowledge of price elasticity that led JetFast to the idea of introducing a budget airline as the company focuses on cost minimisation and the lowest possible price in order to attract customers. As a result, it became the leading budget airline.

ⓔ **5/5 marks awarded.** A good answer providing a clear understanding of elasticity and set fully in the context of JetFast.

Questions & Answers

(c) The product life cycle is an analytical tool that can be used in decision-making in order to help reduce risk. The phases of the plc are introduction, growth, maturity and decline and a knowledge of this can help to determine the marketing policies of a business. A business would have different strategies depending on the stage of the life cycle.

It would appear that JetFast has gone through the phases of introduction and growth and has now entered the maturity phase of the life cycle where it is faced with a number of competitors. Knowing this can help Hal with his decision-making. Competing businesses seem to be developing their service and have been successful in stealing market share from JetFast. He needs to develop JetFast's service in some way; this could be seen as an extension strategy, perhaps offering additional facilities to make the service better or giving greater emphasis to customer service, which seems to be a real problem compared to what its competitors offer.

A knowledge of the product life cycle can therefore benefit the business in terms of the type of marketing and strategy that is adopted — in this case, an extension strategy is necessary.

ℯ 9/9 marks awarded. The first paragraph demonstrates a good understanding of the product life cycle and the second paragraph shows how this knowledge could be useful to JetFast. The answer is set in the context of the business and the analysis is well developed. The final sentence merely sums up the action needed in this case.

(d) The marketing mix is the 7Ps and in order to develop a marketing strategy they should be fully integrated in any marketing plan. This is likely to mean that no one element can claim to be the most important.

In the past, price may have been an important element of the mix for JetFast as the notion of a budget airline implies that price is a key factor. Even so, unless the product or service is good, customers are unlikely to base a decision on price alone. Therefore, although price was low customers would also prioritise safety so the planes used would need to be new and up to date. The airline would also need to serve routes customers wanted.

Present circumstances appear to suggest that price is not the only aspect considered by customers. The competition is gaining market share from JetFast as a result of offering a better all-round service, so the Ps of people and process are becoming increasingly important in the budget airline industry.

In evaluation, although price is an important part of a budget airline's marketing mix, it cannot be termed the most important as it is the right combination of all the Ps that make a good marketing strategy. The product has to be right, with correct routes and modern planes, the business requires promotion and the customer service also has to be spot-on (people and process).

🅮 **13/15 marks awarded.** A good answer. The proposition is put forward in the opening paragraph that no single element of the marketing mix is going to be the most important and this is supported and justified throughout the answer. Although the analysis could be further developed, the response is fully in context.

> **(e)** By other functional areas Hal is referring to other departmental areas besides marketing, such as operations and people. If JetFast is to regain its position, it does seem that action is necessary. A new marketing strategy might help to improve things by perhaps undertaking further development of its product to make it more appealing to the customer, but this alone may not be enough to attract customers back.
>
> Maybe the airline needs to look more closely at its operations and in particular its customer service. Its image is one of cost-cutting by charging for the toilets and extra baggage. This is not going to attract customers to them. Customers expect a certain level of customer service where they are treated well and looked after, and this is what makes them return as customers.
>
> Good customer service is also about having motivated staff: if employees are not motivated, they are unlikely to treat customers well. Staff at JetFast do not have the best conditions of work, having to pay for uniforms and not having guaranteed hours because of zero hours contracts. If JetFast wants to improve customer service, perhaps it should first look at improving employee working conditions.
>
> Overall, Hal is probably correct in saying JetFast has to look at other functional areas such as operations and people, although these areas have come to be part of the 7Ps of marketing in that process and people are now included.

🅮 **11/16 marks awarded.** This student has fully grasped the issues of this question, recognising that functional areas such as people and operations management are important. Consideration is given to these areas in the second and third paragraphs, as well as marketing in the first paragraph. Although the arguments might benefit from further development, they are set consistently in the context of JetFast. The conclusion also has some justification but, as with the analysis, more could have been done.

🅮 **Total score: 43/50 marks = a top grade A. Although the response to part (e) is a little weaker than the other questions, this is an excellent response overall that would have little problem achieving a grade A.**

Student B

> **(a)** Qualitative market research is a form of primary market research that uses focus groups to collect the opinions of customers and potential customers. Such research would enable JetFast to collect information about its service and ideas of how to improve it. This might enable the airline to regain its position as the leading budget airline.

Questions & Answers

There is a clear understanding of qualitative market research here, but the application is somewhat limited.

(b) Elasticity of demand measures the responsiveness of demand to a change in a variable. Demand may be either elastic or inelastic and a knowledge of this could be useful to JetFast in terms of pricing its service. If demand is price elastic, it means it can lower its price and achieve greater sales and profit as a result.

This is a theoretical answer. Elasticity is understood, but it is not explained in terms of JetFast. Suggesting that if demand is price elastic prices can be lowered is not specific application to the business as this is true for any business with elastic products.

(c) Development, introduction, growth, maturity and decline are the five stages of the product life cycle and a knowledge of where a product or service is in its life cycle can help with decision-making in business. For example, in the introductory stage large amounts will need to be spent on marketing to create consumer awareness, whereas in the maturity phase efforts may be more focused on developing extension strategies to maintain a high level of sales. The benefits of this are that a business such as JetFast is able to maximise its sales and therefore profit at all times. When linked with other tools such as the Boston Matrix, this enables a business to establish the best marketing strategies to suit the company and therefore maximise sales.

This is a theoretical answer that correctly explains how a knowledge of the product life cycle could help in business decision-making. There is no attempt to set this in the context of JetFast.

(d) It is clear that what makes a budget airline is the price it charges; people use its service because of the prices. If it charges higher prices, they would just use a regular airline. Price therefore is definitely the most important element of any budget airlines marketing mix. When using a budget airline, people are aware that they have to pay extra for bags and food and so are not expecting the service to be particularly great — as long as they get from A to B that is their main concern. This is true especially today when money is tight due to recession and lack of pay rises meaning that price is going to be the most important factor to anyone travelling on a budget airline. If they could afford to pay more, they would use a regular airline.

This answer focuses solely on price. It has some context for the argument made and would earn some reward. However, there is nothing to suggest that this student actually understands what is meant by the marketing mix and as a result the response lacks balance and any justification to the claim made.

(e) Hal is correct — a complete rethink is necessary. JetFast's market has become increasingly competitive and it is losing market share and action is needed to halt the slide. Other airlines are offering more than just low price; they are offering greater convenience and better customer service and he needs to halt the slide. Changing the marketing strategy and altering the mix might help, but this may not be enough.

Maybe routes need to change to fly to major city airports rather than airports miles from anywhere. Having more routes to more convenient airports would certainly be more attractive to customers. Maybe Hal needs to look at customer service as consumers don't just look for price today; they do expect a certain level of customer service and to be treated politely and as individuals. Perhaps if one item of hold luggage went free this might help or if a free cup of tea or coffee were offered.

In evaluation, Hal needs to look at more than just the marketing mix if JetFast is to regain its position as the leading budget airline. All areas of the business need to be covered to make sure any plan is fully integrated.

ⓔ **6/16 marks awarded.** This student has made a judgement, but there is no clear indication that there is any understanding of what is meant by functional areas despite the direct reference in the final sentence of the case study. When discussing routes this is perhaps product, and customer service has been taken from the text rather than referring specifically to operations management. Some reward would be given for this as there is some context, but there is little in the way of a developed argument and the judgement made has little, if any, justification.

ⓔ **Total score: 22/50 marks = a low pass grade. Overall, a weak response that would struggle to achieve a pass grade. The best that could be hoped for is a grade E.**

Essay questions (A-level)

Question 1

A large manufacturing business is considering the introduction of new technology into its production process, resulting in inevitable job losses. To what extent do you believe that conflict between different stakeholder groups is inevitable in these circumstances?

(25 marks)

Student A

A stakeholder is anyone who has an interest in the business and could be shareholders, employees, local community, government etc. To some extent, conflict between stakeholder groups is inevitable as it is almost impossible to keep everyone happy all of the time and different stakeholders have different objectives. Shareholders are interested in profit whereas employees are more interested in working conditions and job security. a

In the situation in this question, conflict is highly likely as the introduction of new technology will result in a number of redundancies meaning workers will fear for their job security and may become demotivated as a result. Shareholders, on the other hand, are likely to be happy as new technology could mean significant cost reductions in the future, better quality products and higher profits. If quality is better, customers will be happier and this could lead to improved reputation and higher sales, resulting in even happier shareholders. b

The conflict of interest between shareholders and employees does not however have to be inevitable and it depends on a number of factors. This might be how the decision to introduce technology is communicated to the workforce and how it is implemented. If there is a culture of continuous improvement in the business and if the workforce is kept fully involved with the decision-making process, they are more likely to accept the decision. If it is implemented in stages and any redundancies are voluntary rather than forced, it is more likely to be accepted. In practice, however, these types of decisions are often forced on a business by circumstances — such as responding to competitive pressures — and implemented quickly. c

It is also possible for a business such as this to reduce the likelihood of shareholder conflict by using stakeholder mapping. This is the process of analysing stakeholders according to their interest and influence. Therefore, if a business can identify those stakeholders with the most interest and influence in any decisions, they can focus their attention on these in order to reduce the likely impact. d

Overall, conflict between different stakeholder groups is in most cases inevitable as different stakeholders have different interests and decisions tend to be implemented quickly rather than phased in. If all stakeholders are fully involved with the decision, this is less likely to be the case. e

e a The opening paragraph lays the foundations of this essay, demonstrating both an understanding of stakeholders and the issues involved in the question. It also suggests a judgement that hopefully will be supported through the essay. b The second paragraph clearly shows the nature of the potential conflict as a result of the introduction of new technology and recognises that both shareholders and consumers may be happier. c Here, a counter-argument is given and well developed. d A new idea of stakeholder mapping is introduced as a way of trying to avoid conflict. e The final paragraph draws the answer together, suggesting that although it is possible to reduce conflict, in most cases it is inevitable. The initial judgement seems to be well supported throughout the answer.

Overall a solid, well planned and structured essay that would likely achieve a grade B or above.

Student B

Conflict between stakeholder groups in many cases is inevitable especially in this case. Employees are likely to be losing their jobs, so they are not going to be happy. They require job security so will almost certainly conflict with management who want to introduce the new technology. This could even lead to industrial action such as strikes by the workers in order to try to save their jobs. **a**

There is also likely to be conflict between shareholders and employees because shareholders may be quite happy with this decision as it is likely to lead to lower costs and improved profitability. They will be happy with better profits as it is likely to mean higher dividends and even a rising share price. However, employees may be left without a job and have less security in their job. **b**

The local community and the government may not be happy about this decision as it will mean rising unemployment, which means the government will have to pay more in unemployment benefit. The local community will also suffer as there will be less spending in the community due to the lower disposable income which means other businesses will also suffer. **c**

Overall, it does seem this decision will inevitably cause conflict between stakeholders and not just between workers and management. There are many groups that will be affected and will not be happy about this decision. **d**

e **a** The opening paragraph launches straight into the answer, recognising that employees are likely to be upset about such a decision and conflict with management. **b** Next, the potential conflict with shareholders is illustrated. **c** The same is now illustrated for the local community. **d** The conclusion is drawn that conflict is inevitable.

Overall, this answer lacks balance. No consideration has been given to any counter-argument and the judgement made lacks weight and cannot be fully justified. It would probably achieve a low pass grade but no more.

Question 2

To what extent do you believe that the recent growth in popularity of discount retailers is based on the fact that a consumer makes a decision to purchase solely according to the price of a product? Justify your view.   (25 marks)

Student A

The discount retailers include retailers such as Aldi and Primark whose great attraction to customers is the price they charge. The price of their groceries and clothes are significantly cheaper than the likes of Next and Tesco. For some consumers, particularly during the recession, price would have been a significant influence on their decision-making. With less disposable income, they would have looked for cheaper prices. Price would therefore in this case have been the basis for purchase. **a**

If we look at clothing retailers such as Primark, their prices are very low. This is largely due to the fact they source their products overseas often from factories that exploit labour. Women and children are paid minimal wages and work long hours. One factory in Bangladesh even collapsed, killing many workers. Although a few people may have stopped shopping at Primark because of this, they still manage to survive and prosper, suggesting that even though they might be socially irresponsible people shop there because of their low prices and because those prices have a bigger influence than ethics on their decision to buy. b

Although price may be important to consumers in most cases, it is not the only factor they will consider. Quality is also important. Consumers may have moved to Aldi during the recession, but why do they continue to shop there afterwards? It is because they have discovered the quality of the goods are just as good as Tesco? By shopping at Aldi, they are able to achieve greater value for their money — a combination of quality and price. Aldi is able to sell its products cheaper because it cuts costs in other areas such as promotion and extravagant displays, not because it compromises on quality. c

The same might be said for Primark. The quality is just as good as Next in many cases, but consumers want to be seen in new clothes and don't always want to wear the same thing. By shopping at Primark, they are able to buy more regularly and keep up to date with fashion, suggesting it is not only the price that influences their decision. d

Overall, price is a significant factor in a consumer's decision to purchase from discount retailers, particularly if they continue to buy when these retailers have been found to be exploiting workers in developing countries. However, this is too simplistic a view. Consumers also look for quality and value for money, suggesting it is not only price that determines a purchase. e

e a The student gets straight into the answer, suggesting that during recessionary times price plays a big role in a decision to purchase. b This is reinforced using the example of Primark to show that price is more important than ethics. c and d Counter-arguments are now made, showing that consumers also base their decision on factors such as quality and fashion. Having switched to discount retailers, they have found the quality is just as good in Aldi as in Tesco. e The final conclusion that although price is important other factors are also considered seems to be supported throughout the essay.

Overall, a well-balanced essay that shows signs good planning and would likely achieve at least a B grade.

Student B

Consumers today are much more likely to base a decision to buy on price. This is because the internet and social media have made consumers far more price-aware. Before making a purchase, they are likely to Google a product to find the cheapest price online and, even if they then go to a shop, they are likely to negotiate a price with the shop manager based on what they have seen on the net. Although discount retailers are more likely sell groceries and clothes rather than consumer durables, the consumer is still likely to make a purchase on price. a

Discount retailers such as Aldi have grown in popularity over recent years. They sell regular grocery products at prices much cheaper than regular supermarket chains, so consumers can make considerable savings on their household shopping. Although discounters tend to not always have the range of products of supermarkets and their decor is less inviting, people still go there because of the prices — even if they have to queue at the checkouts for ages as I have had to in the past. If the products are exactly the same, why pay more? b

For some products, however, consumers are prepared to pay more such as the iPhone. This is because of the reputation of Apple. It is trendy to own an Apple product — everyone wants the latest product and people are happy to pay a higher price. Discount retailers don't sell this kind of product, so consumers have to pay the high price. Therefore, for some products price is not the key factor in making a purchase. c

Overall, I believe that the growth in discount retailers is due to consumers attaching the highest priority to price when making a decision. d

e a The first paragraph raises an important issue about the greater price awareness of consumers, but it is not developed in relation to the question as shown by the student's own recognition in the last sentence. b The next paragraph suggests that discount retailers are less convenient, so it must be price that attracts people. This is a valid point, but the development is limited. c The answer now drifts from the question. Other factors are important, but the development here is not relevant to discount retailers. d Finally, the overall conclusion is weak and lacking in support.

Overall, this essay raises some important issues, but it does not have a clear focus on the exact question set perhaps because of a lack of planning. The answer would struggle to achieve a pass grade.

Quantitative skills question practice (AS and A-level)

Questions 1 and 2 provide examples of the type of calculation you might be required to undertake in relation to costs, revenue and profit. As these questions are about manipulating the data, you will be given certain information from which other information can be calculated. For example, you may not be given the revenue figure, but with the price per unit and output you should be able to calculate this.

Questions 3 to 6 relate to market share, market growth and market size. Here, you are given certain information from which you are expected to calculate further information. Once again, it is about manipulating the data provided.

Question 7 gives an example of what you might be expected to do in relation to decision trees.

Questions & Answers

Question 1

From the information below, calculate:

(a) Revenue.

(b) Variable cost per unit.

(c) Total costs.

(d) Profit.

Price per unit	£2.50
Total variable costs	£150,000
Fixed costs	£75,000
Output	120,000 units

Question 2

From the information below, calculate:

(a) Total variable costs.

(b) Total costs.

(c) Fixed costs.

(d) Price per unit.

Variable cost per unit	£3.00
Revenue	£5.5m
Output	1.5m units
Profit	£0.5m

Question 3

From the information below, calculate:

(a) Sales turnover.

(b) Market share.

ⓔ Note that the term 'sales turnover' used here this is exactly the same as sales revenue.

Price per unit	£4.00
Output	12.5m units
Total market sales	£224m

Question 4

From the information below, calculate:

(a) Market growth.

(b) Company X sales growth.

(c) Market share in 2012.

(d) What do you think will have happened to market share of Company X in 2014 and why? Confirm your answer by calculation.

	2012	2013
Market size	£500m	£560m
Company X sales	£25m	£25.8m

Question 5

If Company Y's sales are £53m and it has a 16% market share, what is the total value of the market?

Question 6

The sales of Company Z increased by 5% in 2014 to £53m. What was the value of sales in 2013?

Question 7

Using the decision tree below, answer the following questions.

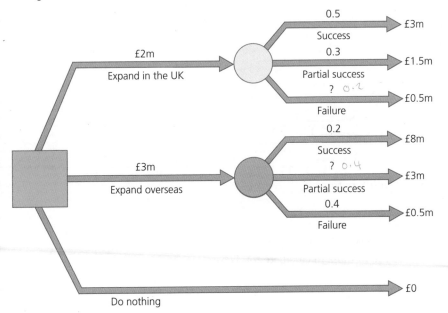

Company X is looking to grow its business and has choice between expanding its UK market or expanding overseas.

(a) What is the probability of failure in the UK?

(b) What is the probability of partial success overseas?

(c) Using numerical data only, which decision should be undertaken?

Answers to quantitative skills question practice

Note that all answers are given to two decimal points and in each case indicate units (for example, m), value (for example, £) or percentage (%). It is essential you also show these in your final answers. Not doing so could cost you a mark. It is also essential that all working is shown as credit will be given for this. For example, if you make one mathematical error and just put down an answer you will get no marks, but if your workings are there and the calculation is undertaken correctly, you might lose only 1 mark.

Question 1

(a) Revenue = price per unit x output
$$= 2.5 \times 120{,}000$$
$$= £300{,}000$$

(b) Variable cost per unit $= \dfrac{\text{total variable costs}}{\text{output}}$
$$= \dfrac{150{,}000}{120{,}000}$$
$$= £1.25$$

(c) Total costs = fixed costs + variable costs
$$= 75{,}000 + 150{,}000$$
$$= £225{,}000$$

(d) Profit = revenue – total costs
$$= 300{,}000 - 225{,}000$$
$$= £75{,}000$$

Question 2

(a) Total variable costs = variable cost per unit × output
$$= 3 \times 1.5m$$
$$= £4.5m$$

(b) Profit is calculated as revenue minus total costs. As we have the figures for both revenue and profit, we can manipulate the formula to calculate total costs.

Total costs = revenue – profit
$$= 5.5m - 0.5m$$
$$= £5m$$

(c) Total costs are calculated as fixed costs plus variable costs. As we now have the figures for both total costs and variable costs, we can now work out fixed costs.

Fixed costs = total costs – variable costs

$$= 5m - 4.5m$$
$$= £0.5m$$

(d) Price per unit = $\dfrac{\text{revenue}}{\text{output}}$

$$= \dfrac{5.5m}{1.5m}$$
$$= £3.66$$

Question 3

(a) Sales turnover = price per unit × output

$$= 4 \times 12.5$$
$$= £50m$$

(b) Market share = $\dfrac{\text{sales (revenue)}}{\text{total market sales}} \times 100$

$$= \dfrac{50}{224} \times 100$$
$$= 22.32\%$$

Question 4

(a) Market growth = $\dfrac{\text{current market size} - \text{previous market size}}{\text{previous market size}} \times 100$

$$= \dfrac{560 - 500}{500} \times 100$$
$$= 12\%$$

(b) Company X sales growth = $\dfrac{\text{current sales figure} - \text{previous sales figure}}{\text{previous sales figure}} \times 100$

$$= \dfrac{25.8 - 25}{25} \times 100$$
$$= 3.2\%$$

(c) Market share = $\dfrac{\text{sales (revenue)}}{\text{total market sales}} \times 100$

$$= \dfrac{25}{500} \times 100$$
$$= 5\%$$

(d) Market share will have declined further by 2014 as Company X sales growth is lower than market growth.

$$\text{Market share in 2013} = \frac{\text{sales (revenue)}}{\text{total market sales}} \times 100$$

$$= \frac{25.8}{560} \times 100$$

$$= 4.6\%$$

Question 5

$$\text{Total market sales} = \frac{\text{sales (revenue)}}{\text{market sales}} \times 100$$

$$= \frac{53m}{16} \times 100$$

$$= £331.25m$$

Question 6

Sales in 2014 were 105% (2013 represents 100% + 5% increase). Therefore, divide this year's sales by 105 to arrive at a figure for 1% and then multiply this by 100 for the 2013 sales figure.

$$\text{Sales in 2013} = \frac{53m}{105} \times 100$$

$$= £50.47m$$

Question 7

(a) The probability of failure in the UK is 0.2.

(b) The probability of partial success overseas is 0.4.

(c) Expand in the UK $= (3 \times 0.5) + (1.5 \times 0.3) + (0.5 \times 0.2) - 2$
$$= 1.5 + 0.45 + 0.1 - 2$$
$$= £50,000$$
Expand overseas $= (8 \times 0.2) + (3 \times 0.4) + (0.5 \times 0.4) - 3$
$$= 1.6 + 1.2 + 0.2 - 3$$
$$= £0$$

Therefore, Company X would be better off expanding within the UK.

Knowledge check answers

1 To make money, to provide goods and services and to provide help and support to others.

2 The mission statement paints the broad picture whereas the objectives are more specific. Objectives are targets or goals that enable the business to achieve its overall mission.

3 SMART means business objectives should be specific, measurable, achievable, realistic and time-based.

4 Three advantages of a sole trader include: they are easy to set up, the owner takes all the profit and their affairs remain private.

5 An incorporated business has limited liability and is recognised as a separate entity in the eyes of the law whereas an unincorporated business does not have a separate legal status from its owners and has unlimited liability.

6 A mutual is a business that is established for the benefit of its members who collectively own the business. Examples include building societies and insurance companies which were traditionally organised in this way.

7 The ease of setting up, the risk involved and the product or service offered.

8 The share price might fall because of falling profit, the expectation of falling profit or general economic uncertainty.

9 Market capitalisation represents the value of a business and is calculated as share price × number of shares issued.

10 A business might benefit from a fall in interest rates through increased demand because of greater disposable income of consumers as a result of lower interest payments on loans and mortgages. The business itself might also benefit from lower interest payments on any loans, thereby reducing costs.

11 A business might adopt a fair-trade approach to enhance its reputation as an ethical business, which could generate greater sales.

12 The role of a manager includes setting objectives, analysing, making decisions, reviewing and leading.

13 Autocratic, democratic and laissez faire.

14 The Tannenbaum Schmidt continuum shows the relationship between the level of freedom a manager chooses to give a team and the level of authority of the manager. The Blake Mouton grid, on the other hand, is a method of analysing leadership styles in terms of a leader's concern for people and concern for task.

15 The choice of decisions to be made and their cost, the probability of success for each decision and the payoff or financial outcome for each probability.

16 This is the systematic approach of collecting facts and applying logical decision-making techniques. It uses analytical tools such as decision trees instead of generalising, trial and error, guessing or using gut feeling.

17 Consumers, employees, shareholders, suppliers, the local community and national government.

18 Stakeholder mapping helps to identify the most influential and powerful stakeholders involved in a decision. Once identified, a business can then focus its attentions on these groups in order to achieve success.

19 Sales value is the amount of sales in £s and sales volume is the number of sales in units.

20 Internal influences include finance available and expertise of personnel, whereas external influences include the economy and actions of competitors.

21 Market share refers to the proportion of total sales in a market controlled by one business, for example Tesco may control 28% of the grocery food market.

22 Qualitative data refers to the opinions and views of consumers collected through methods such as focus groups, whereas quantitative data refers to statistical data collected through surveys.

23 Sampling is important because it is impossible to question all consumers. A small representative group is interviewed with the assumption they will reflect the views of the whole market. Sampling is a cost-effective method of collecting market research information.

24 Correlation refers to the extent to which two or more variables fluctuate together, for example there might be a positive correlation between the sales of a business and the amount of advertising undertaken.

25 Demand would fall, as would revenue and profit.

26 The Boston Matrix is used in product portfolio analysis and shows a product in terms of its potential market growth and market share.

27 Skimming pricing is setting a high price in order to skim off profit and an example is its use for new innovative products. Penetration pricing is the setting of a low price in order to gain entry into a market and an example is a new magazine launch.

28 A combination of the promotional methods used for a product or group of products and includes advertising, direct marketing, personal selling, POS displays and merchandising.

29 E-commerce refers to the buying and selling of products and services through an electronic medium.

30 These Ps have become important because in the service industry the people involved with selling the product, the way it is sold and the physical environment in which it is sold are crucial to the success of a business. A manufacturer needs to consider these aspects as the way its product is sold and the physical environment in which it is sold can have a big impact on the level of sales.

31 In the growth stage the emphasis is on building a brand that differentiates a product from its competitors, whereas in the maturity stage efforts focus on building and maintaining customer loyalty with perhaps special promotions and incentives.

32 Lower costs owing to not having retail stores and a wider market as in theory the business can be global.

Index

Index